The Pillars of the Post-Pandemic Knowledge-Driven Economy: Research Findings

Written by

Mostafa Sayyadi & Mike Provitera

Copyright © September 28, 2021, Dr. Michael Provitera.

All rights reserved. No part of this publication may be reproduced, distributed, or transmitted in any form or by any means, including photocopying, recording, or other electronic or mechanical methods, without the prior written permission of Dr. Michael Provitera, except in the case of brief quotations embodied in critical reviews and certain other noncommercial uses permitted by copyright law.

For permission requests, write to Dr. Michael Provitera @ **docprov@msn.com**, with the subject title addressed "***Attention: Permissions Coordinator***," and visit **http://docprov.com** for free workbooks, podcasts, and videos.

ISBN: 9798534512878 (Paperback)
ISBN: **To Be Announced in September 2021** (E-book)

Library of Congress Control Number: 2001

Any references to historical events, real people, or real places are used fictitiously. Names, characters, and places are products of the author's imagination unless otherwise documented.
Front cover image created by Dr. Mostafa Sayyadi
Book designed by Dr. Michael Provitera
Line-by-Line Editing by Dr. Michael Provitera
Printed by Motivational Leadership Training, Inc., in the United States of America. Website: **http://docprov.com/hire-mike.html**
For Management Consulting, Contact Dr. Mike: 954-613-3903

Contents

Preface
Introduction
Foreword
Case Study

Chapter 1: **The Post-Pandemic Horizon: A Knowledge-Driven Economy**

Chapter 2: **Organizational Challenges in a Post-Pandemic World**

Chapter 3: **Post-Pandemic Recovery with Technology And Knowledge Management**

Chapter 4: **Post-Pandemic Recovery Using Human Resource Technology**

Chapter 5: **Post-Pandemic Recovery Strategy Formulation**

Chapter 6: **Transformational Leadership Development in a Post-pandemic World**

Chapter 7: **Transformational Leadership, Knowledge Management and Company Performance**

Chapter 8: **Operational Risk Management in The Post-Pandemic**

Featured Case Study: **Tesla, A Knowledge Management Think Tank**

References

PREFACE

Are knowledge-management leaders more effective? Are knowledge-management workers more productive and satisfied? Studies of knowledge-management, which have been taken in a range of fields, have implications for a wide variety of topics in organizational behavior and human resource management. Yet, this research has been scattered, resulting in only anecdotal evidence of managerial application. We review the organizational behavior and leadership literature to distinguish, propose, and assess research of knowledge-management coupled with transformational leadership as both process and content. Our synthesis of past research on the content of knowledge-management and transformational leadership is organized around five distinct pillars: ***Culture, structure, strategy, networks, and stakeholders.*** Our book concludes with an evaluation of the implications of our findings for future research in knowledge-management, organizational behavior, human resource management, and transformational leadership.

Foreword

Introduction

Transformational leadership is described as an inspirational role that managers can apply to enhance the organization's intellectual capital and ultimate performance. The question arises whether transformational leadership itself is a source of effectiveness in the post-pandemic world. This basic question remains unexplored to date. Based upon this gap in empirical research, the purpose of this book is to synthesize the extant literature on transformational leadership and knowledge management in the field of management and organizational behavior and introduce the concept of the post-pandemic recovery. The design of this book is structured to present a framework that explains the theoretical linkage among organizational factors in the post-pandemic economy. Managerial applications that may support knowledge-driven performance are proposed here but further research is necessary to finalize conclusions. Thus, the practical implication of this book provides scenarios for executives to consider as possible causal relationships among various organizational factors in the post pandemic world.

Our contribution to the management and organizational behavior literature lies in presenting a conceptual framework that incorporates the organizational factors that may impact knowledge-driven performance. The findings in this book are based upon previous empirical studies.

This book also has several implications for research. First, given the emphasis in the literature on transformational leadership and knowledge management as two significant indicators for knowledge-driven performance, this book adds to a relatively small body of the post-pandemic recovery literature.

Second, this book advances the current literature on transformational leadership by offering novel insights into how transformational leaders prepare businesses for the new economic recovery. Particularly, we argue that transformational leaders are those managers who effectively exert the necessary changes within organizations. Drawing from the current organizational theories (i.e. social capital view and knowledge-based view), this book suggests new insights to identify transformational leadership as a primary driver, which influences organizational resources. The review of the prior research findings reveal that transformational leaders leverage sizable influence on workplace design. These findings provide evidence that a transformational leadership framework is the kind of workplace model that continues to be resilient and help organizations recovery from the post-COVID era. Third, this book contributes to research on organizational change, through articulating the impact of transformational leadership on organizational design.

The post-pandemic has added rich research and writing opportunities that are needed to help the world recover from the pandemic. For example, how do workers learn centricity, being that the center of an organization is no longer in a building and may be a remote set of landscapes while many employees are still working from home?

How do leaders keep employees engaged and what is the best way to manage group-centered discussions regarding strategic initiatives and concurrent business issues?

What is the impact of spending long hours on the computer while forfeiting the face-to-face meetings with co-workers and clients which, in the past, has be the focal point of business?

What is the post-pandemic impact on family and children of the workers as they work remotely or those who are returning to work in the office while having children at home?

How do employees balance a work-life interface and is it an important concern for executives?

Has the primary responsibility of the post-pandemic recovery been placed on senior management leadership during COVID times?

We attempt to address these questions, but we concur that the post-pandemic recovery is an iterative process and research, inquiry, and observation is ongoing.

Chapter 1: The Post-Pandemic Horizon: A Knowledge-Driven Economy

In the post pandemic economy, only the knowledgeable will survive. Today the psychclogical contracts have changed between leaders and followers as a result of COVID-19. Remote work has risen as the most predominant concern along with keeping stakeholders safe during the pandemic. For example, Bankers that once reported to Manhattan, New York, are home making lunch for themselves as they work remotely from a home-based silo.

The post-pandemic recovery has created hybrid leadership models that incorporate both in-office and –remote communication. Electronic meetings have experienced real-time think tanks that have exploited knowledge management as the world recovers from the pandemic. We pose six questions that get to the heart and mind of the post-pandemic recovery. Answering these questions is indicative of the new mindset today and provides a personal experience.

1. What type of cultural shifts have you made?
2. What type of structural shifts have you made?
3. What type of strategic shifts have you made?
4. What type of technological shifts have you made?
5. What type of relational shifts have you made?
6. Why are these shifts affecting your knowledge-driven performance?

The importance of organizational resources is escalated in the post-pandemic recovery. Organizational resources have led to a new look at resilience as a strategic organizational recovery from COVID-19. This chapter, which is based on our interviews with 179 executives, explains the better use of organizational resources to formulate a vision of knowledge-driven performance improvement for the post-pandemic recovery.

The Pillars of Post-Pandemic Knowledge-Driven Economy

In a post-pandemic world, the business environment is constantly changing. [1] [2] Knowledge is a crucial part of hypercompetitive environments. [3] Due to new advances in technology, organizations can design, copy, or update products and services easier with more adaptability then ever today. Organizations compete globally but must think locally if they expect to succeed. [4] [5] New advances in market trends place demands on the roles of change leaders in organizations operating in this modern environment.

The knowledge-driven economy is placing more pressure on organizations to employ effective leaders who are capable to develop knowledge-based organizations. [6] [7] [8] There are many academic studies that focus on the organizational and managerial factors that drive knowledge-driven performance. [9] [10] [11] [12] [13] Culture, structure, strategy, networks, and stakeholders are such areas that play a critical role and are a strategic prerequisite for business success in the post-pandemic knowledge-driven economy. We have expressed a strong dialogue of these concepts in this book, and we propose that there are limitations to the vast array of knowledge that can be encapsulated to circumvent the pandemic and we emphasize the critical role of strategic initiatives. Our focus is to shed light on the tenets of strategic management that we pose above without stating that these are the only concerns in the Post-Pandemic Recovery.

Pillar 1: Trust-based Culture

Executives have found that a collaborative culture improves the knowledge management process. The executive's ability to create new knowledge and develop more innovative solutions is considerably dependent on the degree to which employees trust them to not only create initiatives but to improve innovation and creative ideas as well. [14] By creating an organization that exhibits a sense of trust throughout the working environment, this positively influences the tendency of human capital to continue to share their knowledge with others. Learning becomes more fluent and viable in a knowledge management culture based upon trusting relationships. Learning, the essence of continuous improvement, is an important requisite for knowledge creation. [15] Firms that stress cultural aspects of learning are stronger in creating new knowledge and they exhibit a tendency to transfer this knowledge throughout the organization. [16] Therefore, with pillar one, we propose that organizational culture is positively associated with knowledge management.

Pillar 2: Agile Strategy

Executives have found that an "Analysis Strategy" may act as an important component of our model to improve company performance. Analysis strategy is defined as the degree or tendency to search for possible problems and their roots aimed at generating better solutions and alternatives to solve them. [17] Analysis strategy is highly related to an organization's capacity to generate new ideas and knowledge. Executives today are remaining to be as proactive as possible in our turbulent and every-changing world economy. Searching for, and finding, new opportunities and responding to current challenges in external environments is key to an organization's success in the post-pandemic. [18] Thus, the implementation and application of a knowledge management system requires the continuous search for novel ideas, structures, and products that appeal to the turbulent business environment that we all face today in our global economy. To remain proactive reduces possible stressors that may influence company performance. [19] As a result, proactiveness strategic management can be critical for enhancing the performance of knowledge management projects in organizations. A more defensiveness approach enhances efficiency through cutting the costs of the potentiality of future problems that may occur when an organization remains reactive to environmental concerns. Many organizations were presented with pandemic related concerns and non-programmatic decisions had to be made swiftly for survival.

Being reactive, and in some cases such as COVID-19, propels the process of knowledge reuse in companies, which may lead to stale and unwarranted information. [20] Based upon this assumption, with pillar two, we propose that organizational analysis-strategy is positively associated with knowledge management.

Pillar 3: Flexible Structure

Decentralization, sometimes referred to as organic or teamwork, is known to encourage organizational communication, and develop a climate of openness for employees to exchange new ideas. At Salomon Brothers, we restructured traditional functions into team-based functions and the communication increased dramatically.

Employees at lower echelons of organizations can implement ideas through delegating the authority of decision-making throughout their departments. This type of empowerment and autonomy is warranted not only pre- and post-pandemic, but also for any organization at any time.

An organic structure enhances organizational communication, and the less emphasis on formal organizational protocol and the cultural-language itself could generate more knowledge, because formal procedures and rules can restrict the generation of new ideas. Centralized decision-making may work in a static and controlled environment while decentralized structures may enhance organizational communication in a more dynamic and turbulent environment. Are we in a turbulent environment today as we face the post-pandemic recovery? I am sure that your answer is yes as we all face an unprecedented global pandemic.

Scholars conducted empirical research that investigated the impact of these structural aspects, decentralization, and centralized decision-making, on various knowledge management processes such as knowledge acquiring, knowledge creating, knowledge sharing, and most importantly, knowledge utilizing. [17] Based upon these findings, we propose scenario number three that flexible structures are positively associated with knowledge management.

Pillar 4: Technology

Scholars have noticed that an organization's social network enhances knowledge acquisition. [21] The process of storing knowledge is also dependent on the extent to which knowledge is transferred by the organization's social networking. [22] Just the mere transference of knowledge itself can improve knowledge utilization and knowledge creation within organizations. [23] As a result, networks found throughout and within organizations are positively related to the knowledge management.

Pillar 5: Stakeholder orientation

A stakeholder orientation is an important aspect of company performance. Stakeholder orientation is created to enhance the exchange of knowledge with various stakeholders and the application for more effective decision-making. [24] Executives have found that knowledge exchange is experience-based and highly relevant to both context and location, and can facilitate the generation of new knowledge, which represents those decisions and policies created by interacting with various stakeholders. As we approach the post-pandemic with strong communication and an awareness of safety, more executives are working from remote sites or experiencing flexible office hours. Thus, stakeholders play a significant role in the policy-making process as interactions with different facets of the organization play a critical part for creating explicit and implicit knowledge. [25] Thus, we propose the fifth, and last scenario, as the significant role of stakeholders in knowledge management.

Prior Research with Indicative Examples for Executives

With the pandemic almost over, executives are managing knowledge and using new, coupled with past knowledge, as an important driving force for business success. While the outcome of a pandemic is not always positive, some executives are finding that their organization may be more competitive and on the cutting edge due the insurmountable changes made in a short period of time to augment the worldwide pandemic. Workers had to adapt to the new procedures such as but not limited to online meetings, remote leadership, and collaboration by phone, text, and instant message. On a positive note, some may feel that this phrase, **Roaring Covid Nineteens'** which we coin for the purpose of this book, may demonstrate how one feels after surviving such a crisis. However, this term, as positive as it is, may be a shortsighted realization as the pandemic has a lingering effect on the global marketplace.

Given the situation as of August 2021, a year, and a half since the acknowledgement of the pandemic, the coronavirus has caused a huge disruption in the lives of people and the way they conduct purchases, how they work, and the way they engage with society. Organizations around world managed many changes and will continue to do so in the post-pandemic recovery. With the impact of remote work and the gradual return to the office, organizations are still attempting to prevent the spread of the virus. The increased spread of COVID-19 continues to create uncertainty about the timelines for returning to the office and executives are barring the new highly transmittable COVID-19 Delta variant.

Attempting to remain positive and work on a post-pandemic recovery, there are, however, some critical success factors that are noted and exploited using knowledge management implementation in organizations (see Table 1).

We found that executives can develop conducive organizational climates that foster collaboration and organizational learning in which knowledge, as a driver of improved knowledge-driven performance, is shared and exploited. Unshared knowledge is like lettuce in the refrigerator---if eaten and shared, everyone enjoys it, if left untouched, it goes bad and does not have any use.

It is important to stand on the shoulders of the scholars that have found managerial applications that help executives not only during the post-pandemic recovery but also over the last few decades. CEOs also managed to find novel ways to sustain their businesses during the pandemic. The following table (Table 1) addresses previous academic research that identifies the critical success factors for knowledge-driven performance in organizations.

Source	Publication	Critical Success Factors
David Skyrme and Debra Amidon [26]	The Knowledge Agenda	*Knowledge leadership* *Creating a knowledge-sharing culture* *Well-developed technology infrastructure* *Strong link to a business imperative* *Compelling vision and architecture* *Systematic organizational knowledge* *Processes and Continuous learning*
Simon Trussler	The Rules of the Game	*Appropriate infrastructure*

[27]			*Leadership and strategy (management commitment)* *Creating motivation to share.* *Finding the right people and data,* *Culture,* *And Technology (network).* *Availability to collaborators (transferring)* *Training and learning*
Jay Liebowitz [28]		Key Ingredients to the Success of an Organization's Knowledge Management Strategy	*KM strategy with senior leadership support and active involvement* *A CKO or equivalent and a knowledge management infrastructure.*

			Knowledge ontologies and knowledge Repositories. Knowledge systems, tools, and Incentives to encourage knowledge Sharing. Building a supportive culture
APQC [29]		Knowledge Management: Executive Summary, Consortium Benchmarking Study and Best Practice Report	*Leadership Culture. Technology. Strategy. Measurement.*
Clyde Holsapple and Kalpak		An Investigation of Factors that Influence the	*Leadership Coordination, Control, and*

Joshi [30]	Management of Knowledge in Organizations	***Measurement***
Michael Stankosky and Carolyn Baldanza [31]	A Systems Approach to Engineering a Knowledge Management System	***Leadership, Organization, Technology, and Learning***
Kuan Yew Wong [32]	Critical Success Factors for Implementing Knowledge Management In Small and Medium Enterprises	***Management, leadership, and Support. Culture. Information Technology. Strategy and purpose. Measurement. Organizational infrastructure, Processes, and activities.***

		Motivational aids. *Resources.* *Training and education.* *Human resource management*
Yu-Chung Hung and colleagues [33]	Critical Factors in Adopting a Knowledge Management System for the Pharmaceutical Industry	*A trusting and open organizational Culture.* *Senior management, leadership, and Commitment.* *Employee involvement.* *Employee training.* *Trustworthiness and teamwork.* *Employee empowerment* *Information systems.* *Infrastructure.* *Performance measurement.*

		Benchmarking. *Knowledge structure.*
Ying-Jung Yeh and his colleagues [34]	Knowledge Management Enablers: A Case Study	*Strategy and leadership.* *Corporate culture.* *People.* *Information technology.* *Content quality.* *Collaboration.* *Communication.* *Formalization.* *Budgetary support.*
Mahmoud Migdadi [35]	Knowledge Management Enablers and Outcomes in the Small-and-Medium Sized Enterprises	*Management, leadership, and Support.* *Culture.* *Information Technology.* *Strategy and purpose.* *Measurement.*

		Organizational infrastructure. *Processes and activities.* *Motivational aids.* *Resources.* *Training and education.* *Human resource management.*

The Proposed Model

The following figure presents our overall framework that constitutes the conceptual model expressed throughout this book.

TRUST BASED CULTURE. Gilbert W. Fairholm, in his book titled **Leadership and the Culture of Trust**, posited that by "Shaping a culture within which mutual work is done based on mutual interactive trust," in 1994, published by Greenwood Publishing group.

FLEXIBLE STRUCTURE. Scholars, such as Raymond E. Miles, Charles C. Snow, Alan D. Meyer and Henry J. Coleman, Jr. argue that executive's ability to meet successfully

environmental conditions of tomorrow revolves around their understanding of organizations as integrative and dynamic wholes (The Academy of Management Review
Vol. 3, No. 3, July, 1978, pp. 561).

STAKEHOLDERS. In a corporation, a stakeholder is a member of "groups without whose support the organization would cease to exist," as defined in the first usage of the word in a 1963 internal memorandum at the Stanford Research Institute. The theory was later developed and championed by R. Edward Freeman in the 1980s. However, further research indicates that: According to The Oxford English Dictionary (2nd ed., 1991), the word 'stakeholder' first appeared in 1708, meaning the holder of a wager. A stake is 'that which is placed at hazard', although the OED is uncertain where that usage of stake comes from (The Influence Agenda, Mike Clayton, http://Springer.com**)**. Thus, the fact remains that the stakeholder is extremely important to any organization.

TECHNOLOGY. "Organizations and the world in which they exist are undergoing profound changes," states Stewart R Clegg, Cynthia Hardy, and Walter R Nord in ***Managing Organizations Current Issues***, published by *Sage Publications* in 1999.

AGILE STRATEGY. "Now is an opportune time for managers to become more agile and shift their position from one of planning, organizing, staffing, directing, or controlling to one of being a curator, architect, conductor, humanist, advocate, and pioneer," states Michael Edmondson in his book *Agility*, published by *Business Expert Press*, in 2021.

The figure below is indicative of how knowledge

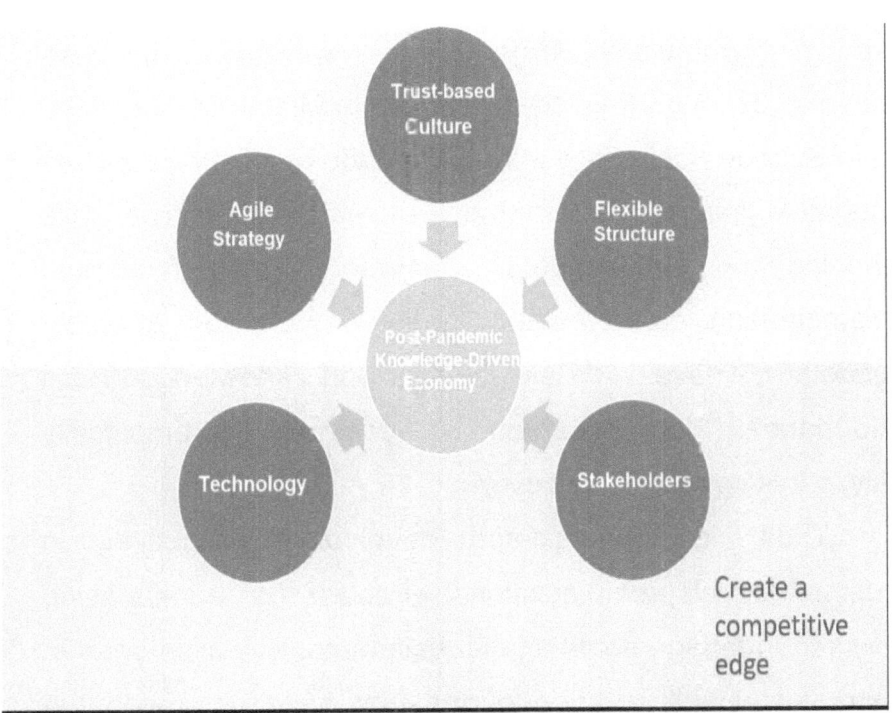

management and transformational leadership come together to influence organizational resources. We relate pertinent dimensions on knowledge-driven performance and extend the extant literature with these scenarios mentioned above. This framework portrays how organizational resources influence knowledge-driven performance. This construct is a new extrapolation from the current research in knowledge-driven performance and can offer a fresh appellation on managerial and executive implication. The **Creating a Competitive Edge** figure has embraced several variables that we have found to be associated in some way with the post-pandemic recovery. **Five Pillars** that continue to be Influencing the knowledge-driven performance of organizations, worldwide, in post-pandemic. Through training executives in Miami Florida, USA, and in Sydney Australia, we found that too much structure had a negative impact on knowledge-driven performance while technology, stakeholders, strategic management implementation, and culture have proven to, at least anecdotally, have positive results on knowledge-driven performance. More research is necessary to empirically analyze this construct, however.

Thus, in training and developing executives in leadership development sessions, we found that leaders using knowledge management techniques attempt to implement and create sustainable change efforts that have embraced the post-pandemic recovery. This brief focus-group study captured as the pandemic subsided and leading to the post-pandemic recover, is based on the following factors:

- Continuing to measure engagement of followers on a quarterly basis, not just on a yearly basis which is currently the norm, this can be employed as a Management By Objectives (MBO) approach or a 360-degree process. We found that a 360-degree process works best and should be used at least once per year;
- Creating action plans with a steering committee that involve key players throughout the organization is important due to the lack of communication and skill-gap of remote work versus the office setting;
- Executives should meet with CEOs as often as possible to discuss current business practices, risk management, and knowledge gathering, knowledge storing, and, most importantly, knowledge dissemination;
- Encourage knowledge management as an annual employee focus group meeting to share ideas and make adjustments and improvements;
- Develop knowledge management systems to hardwire change initiatives and disseminate this information throughout the organization to remain current and up to date on technology platforms throughout not only the organization but also, industry wide.
- Have followers along with leaders participate in incentive-wide activities and committees that help both

internal and external strategic objectives to develop and formulate strategic objective implementation;
- Cut out unnecessary meetings: Create meaningful staff meetings with pre-supposed agenda items and deliverables implemented at the end of the meetings with follow-up when the next meeting begins. Open the next meeting addressing the last meeting deliverables and how they have been met, being worked upon, or need to be carried forward;
- Define follower space and ramp-up accountability to ensure profitable pursuits in an ethical and honest manner, improve follower and employee performance, and enhance employee satisfaction throughout the organization.
- We found that career suppression and career overreach are two concerns of the post-pandemic recovery. In most cases, careers have stability but there is a lack of progression with the remote work setting. Also, the linear career types are encouraging their expert career types to take on leadership roles when the experts are happy to remain at the expert level as they continue to develop their talents.

Chapter Summary

Based upon our contextual framework and derived

model, we emphasize knowledge-driven performance in the post-pandemic world. We provide possible causal relationships that may lead to higher knowledge-driven performance. First, from a financial viewpoint and, second, from an employee satisfaction contingent. This, however, is a result of the recovery from the pandemic. Our premise, in this chapter, is that executives may be able to improve knowledge-driven performance when they incorporate the tenets mentioned in our model.

We see an enhanced use of the most modern knowledge management techniques and we realize that this important facet of organizational performance is affected by various internal characteristics of organizations such as the structure of the organization, the culture of the organization, the strategic planning of the organization, and technology used by the organization. We also found that stakeholders have a strong influence on executive decision-making and company performance relies directly with them.

This chapter, grounded in the knowledge-based view of the firm, presents a framework that may guide future studies in the field of management and organizational behavior. We reveal that there is a lack of empirical support to measure how the dimensions of knowledge-driven performance are facilitated with the effective use of organizational resources. Thus, this chapter is indicative of introducing a model with the intention of a much more developed empirical study. By measuring the five pillars (Trust-based culture, Flexible structure, Stakeholders, Technology, and Agile strategy) introduced in this chapter, future empirical studies may reveal vital information that can help the post-pandemic recovery.

The post-pandemic recovery needs both psychological and empirical research to engage the mind of followers worldwide coupled with leadership decision-making as the world recovers from a year setback that began in March 2020 and still has lingering effects today.

In the knowledge economy, only the knowledgeable will survive. As we continue our research in this area, we welcome our colleagues to use this chapter to further the improvement of knowledge-driven performance.

Chapter 2: Organizational Challenges in a Post-Pandemic World

*I*n this chapter, we highlight how transformational leadership has reshaped knowledge management by blending organizational knowledge and communication with leadership. This marriage has enabled organizations to sustain business process as it continuously changes in a post-pandemic world.

The organizational challenges during the pandemic focused primarily on the organization's internal resources. Technology being the most challenging as many employees had to learn how to use new software for meetings. The stakeholder impact was huge as some customers and vendors could not adapt to the online and remote delivery of products and services. Agility, flexibility, technology, and trust are all important factors for the post-pandemic recovery, and they were also somewhat challenging to manage as executives manifested survival mode to ensure sustainability during the pandemic. These five pillars (stakeholders, agility, flexibility, technology, and trust) will remain operative during the post-pandemic recovery.

An important component of the post-pandemic recovery is the use of transformational leadership coupled with knowledge management. Through articulating the impact of transformational leadership on culture, structure, and strategy, we apply a model that not only emphasizes the role of transformational leadership but also enhances knowledge management. The previous chapter emphasized the importance of knowledge management and this chapter adds transformational leadership as an important tenet for recovery.

Prior to the pandemic, we found insufficient consideration of the impact of transformational leadership on the organization's internal resources. Very little, if any published articles or books have explored how transformational leadership has influenced organizational strategy using both culture and structure as a moderating component. Thus, transformational leadership and the three organizational factors (culture, strategy, and structure) are placed in a model that can be empirically investigated. Thus, this chapter investigates the crossover potential of scholarly research and how it can be applied in the organizational boardroom. Furthermore, we suggest that scholars take our model and conduct research using executives as the focal point so that academic scholarship can meet the needs of managerial implications at the higher echelons of organizations in the post-COVID world. The post-pandemic recovery depends on the research necessary to provide ongoing support to executives as they manage during this turbulent and ever-changing time.

Practical Applications of Prior Research

Organizational Culture

Organizational culture has been defined as a "system of shared values defining what is important, developing norms to help people become familiar with the organization by defining appropriate attitudes and behaviors that guide members' attitudes and actions." [1] In fact, organizational culture is highly reflected in shared assumptions, symbols, beliefs, values and norms, which specifies how employees perceive problems and appropriately react to them. There is considerable alignment between the knowledge-based view of the firm and organizational culture. More specifically, researchers view shared assumptions and values as members' knowledge acquired through learning from others. Scholars subsequently posit that organizational culture can be mobilized to act as a glue to bring workers together and, this notion, when coupled with tapping into the tacit knowledge of workers may be an important strategic factor of competitive advantage. [2] Thus, prior research suggests that it is apparent that organizational culture when considered an internal resource can positively impact competitive advantage through developing shared assumptions and values, which manifest as tacit knowledge embedded in organizational members.

Organizational Structure

Organizational structure refers to the bureaucratic division of labor accompanied by control and coordination between different tasks, in order to develop communication within organizations. [3] Based on the knowledge-based view, knowledge is merely created by people and knowledge application and integration are the most important roles of firms. Accordingly, the capability of companies to integrate individuals' specialized knowledge into products and services can largely generate competitive advantage. A company's structure is an "efficient mechanism for coordinating a complex system comprising multiple specialized units," and should be "structured hierarchically according to the scope of knowledge that they integrate." [4] Hence, the organizational structure reflects an internal resource that is used to integrate intellectual capital and create competitive advantage.

Organizational Strategy

Strategy is a pattern of decisions and plans that are directed at interacting with the corporate environment and efficiently allocating capabilities to achieve organizational objectives. A primary function of strategy is to develop goals and plans to restructure unclear and vague situations into a set of organizationally resolvable problems. As a result, organizational strategies are formed to efficiently deploy the capabilities and interact with environments. Following the knowledge-based view, organizations are social communities that exist to enhance competitive advantage by utilizing and creating new ideas and knowledge. Accordingly, knowledge creation and application manifest themselves as constructs of the knowledge-based view. It is evident that organizational strategy is a sum of objectives, plans, and procedures designed to efficiently upgrade capabilities and interact with the environment, which can assist both paradigms of knowledge utilization and knowledge creation as constructs of the knowledge-based view. In particular, strategy defines a pattern to deploy organizational capabilities and interact with the external environment. Strategic management, therefore, determines how companies should utilize and manage their knowledge assets to create new ideas and knowledge in achieving organizational objectives. Thus, organizational strategy is an internal resource affecting knowledge as an important component for competitive advantage.

Transformational leaders in leading change to better manage organizational knowledge is a secret ingredient for the post-pandemic recovery. The key idea of this secret ingredient is to make the secret explicit and advance the current literature on transformational leadership by offering novel insights into how executives affect an organization's internal resources. Particularly, we feel that the post-pandemic recovery has created a call to executives to enable followers to thrive in the new cultural changes as a result of COVID19, determine more flexible structures, and continuously tweak organizational strategy. Without a grasp on these three tenets during the post-pandemic recovery, executives are bound to fail.

The Post-Pandemic Transformational Leader

Roles changed, not only for the staff of many organizations, but also for the leaders, or as we call here, the executives. Transformational leaders are those executives who engage in the facilitation of building and sustaining relationships with subordinates and this has magnified significantly as the pandemic caused an unprecedented global concern. [5] [6] Executives that embraced transformational leadership with knowledge management had a stronger success rate than those who used other leadership models during the pandemic. Knowledge management, which is as a set of processes aimed at creating value through generating and applying intellectual capital, is significantly enhancing the post-pandemic recovery. [7] We interviewed 48 executives, furthering our view of the mediating effects of the organizational factors than we feel have a strong impact on the post-pandemic recovery (i.e., culture, structure, and strategy). We found a strong relationship between transformational leadership and knowledge management, and perhaps even a marriage. When combining these two theories coupled with the mediating factors (culture structure, and strategy), even tacitly, most executives nodded positively on the impact they have made in the post-pandemic recovery.

The Secret Formula for Post-Pandemic Recovery

In a post pandemic world, culture is projected to include three dimensions: collaboration, trust, and learning. [8] These three key words cannot make or break an organization, but we have found that incorporating each of them together can begin to move an organization toward COVID-19 recovery.

We asked executives how they felt about the role of transformational leadership during the pandemic and now in the post-pandemic recovery. Unanimously, they agreed that transformational leaders enhance collaboration and dialogue by aligning subordinates' individual interests with collective interests of the organization.

With the rise of new technology, trusting a system that is both secure with modern technology will help executives lead now and in the future. [4] Executives that use the transformational leadership model can engender trust by focusing on identifying employees' individual needs within companies and then meeting or exceeding those needs.

Furthermore, most executives agreed with our assumptions found in the literature that transformational leaders provide the freedom for employees to explore new ideas and knowledge. [9] [10] Thus, this leadership style can be applied to develop learning climates. Executives mentioned that they use other models of leadership when engaging with followers. However, our focus is on transformational leadership and how this model has had an impact on the post-pandemic recovery. Because of the nature of the words of transformational leadership, all executives have used this model and mentioned that they will continue to do so.

Executives also mentioned that collaboration is a necessary precursor to create new ideas and knowledge, without collaboration among all levels of the organization, they would not have survived the pandemic. The undeniable reason, they expressed, is being an enabler of extenuating trust-based relationships. This kind of relationships is ideal for sharing tacit knowledge. [11] This is not a novel issue and has surfaced as a scholarly idea for decades. It simply has more application today as we survive the pandemic and prepare for the post-pandemic. In fact, leaders' ability to create knowledge and develop a more innovative climate is a product of employees' trust in their leaders' decisions.

We posit that sharing best practices and experiences (i.e. learning, technology, and presentation equipment) could play a crucial role in embedding organizational knowledge in members and creating new knowledge for companies for the post COVID-19 recovery. Thus, firms emphasizing the cultural aspect of learning are much stronger in generating new ideas and knowledge. Negative connotations and consequences brought upon failed initiatives is shunned and all ideas, good or bad, are welcomed in the post-pandemic recovery. Executives mentioned that if they are to succeed in the post pandemic recovery, it needs to be a concerted and collaborative effort.

Teamwork, sometimes referred to as organic structures, in the workplace, is nothing new and has been a focal point of businesses worldwide for some time now. Peter Drucker once noted that "The Principle of decentralized organizational structures is being expounded in articles and speeches, in management magazines and in management meetings so that by now the phrase at least must be familiar to every American manager," in the Practice of Management, dating back to 1954, page 209. Thus, decentralized structures preceded the pandemic, but we found it became a norm and we do not see this changing in the post-pandemic.

Many leadership models and theories advocate for the decentralized structure, especially in a turbulent environment in which we find ourselves in today with the post-pandemic recovery and international conflict. Since our focus is on transformational leadership, we found that leaders achieve a higher degree of effectiveness in a decentralized structure. [12] The executives, we interviewed, mentioned that an executive acting as a transformational leader develops decentralized structures with the aim of improving knowledge sharing and creating a more innovative climate. Transformational leaders inspire and transform aggregate human capital into social capital in order to implement the required changes to augment the post-pandemic recovery. Highly centralized structures are more bureaucratic, and this negatively contributes to the effectiveness of transformational leadership in changing existing situations.

Decentralization develops a climate of openness for employees to exchange their new ideas. At Salomon Brothers, Inc. in Tampa Florida, executives mandated a new paradigm shift to decentralization and combined several departments to work harmoniously together. The result was better communication, more collaboration, and a much flatter structure.

The pandemic caused decentralization not only from a flatter structure but also from a more electronic one in which email and electronic meetings are the direct link to communication, along with instant messenger, outlook, and text. Pre-meeting and post meeting communication was enhanced with this technology as meetings can be set up with alerts well in advance and reoccurring enablers set up a string of meetings accordingly. Active meetings are utilized as documents are augmented while the meeting is in play. Once executive meetings took place and when the information and clarification is disseminated, then the employees can implement ideas through the delegation of authority of decision-making to their departments to the lowest levels possible and still keep successful execution. [13] [14] [15] Thus, executives pushed decision making down to levels that dealt directly with the customers which is vital for post-pandemic recovery.

We found four tenets of strategy that are undeniably

important to consider. They are analysis, defensiveness, futurity, and pro-activeness. Executives apply analysis strategy to meet the goals of intellectual stimulation, which seeks to provide new and innovative solutions for organizational problems. Analysis strategy was emphasized with resilience as a focal point moving tandem with operational risk management as organizations moved in survival mode. Financial risk management was illuminated but operational risk management superseded as organizations struggled for survival. With the cease of operations, organizations found it challenging to continue to prosper. As the post-pandemic recovery unfolds, transformational leaders are developing a futurity strategy to create a more comprehensive vision for the future. Many mission and vision statements were altered for concurrent pandemic concerns. This was an active response to the pandemic and an operative movement that first surfaced as a safety measure for all. Then other features that impacted the mission statement were implemented such as, but not limited to, remote work and customer response systems. Bill Conerly posited that strategic planning is never easy, in a Forbes article titled, "Business Strategic Planning During The Pandemic: What's Changed, What Hasn't?"

> *Strategic planning is never easy, and it has gotten hugely harder with the Covid-19 pandemic. Baseline forecasts of revenue and costs are tough, and who*

knows whether a second wave or a vaccine will change everything on short order? Yet decisions must be made. The strategic planning process's greatest value may be in identifying uncertainties and options even more than laying out a fixed path for the future. (Conerly, 2020)

We also found that transformational leaders also apply a defensive strategy to implement the required modifications in order to efficiently use organizational resources, decrease costs, and control resources. Thus, taking a proactive approach to inspire employees to investigate better solutions and opportunities. Futurity strategies also use inspirational motivation by setting high expectations and providing a suitable situation for followers to identify new opportunities. These four tenets (analysis, defensiveness, futurity, and proactiveness) of strategic initiatives are predominant today.

The C-Suite regards strategy as an ongoing process, iterative, and without no end in sight as they solve problems and find their root causes and rule them out, and as we noticed during the pandemic, and now, in the post pandemic, they, generate better alternatives to solve concurrent problems. [16] [17]

Analysis strategy could play a critical role in accumulating organizational knowledge, including both processes of knowledge creation and knowledge acquisition.

We found that proactive strategy has positively

contributed to knowledge management performance through developing interactions with external environments as the pandemic became a huge concern worldwide. As the post-pandemic recovery comes to fruition, executives realize that effective implementation of knowledge management projects require a continuous investigation from external business environments that are also dealing with the impact of COVID-19.

Defensiveness is an approach that enhances efficiency through reusing knowledge to reduce organizational costs. [14] Working together with Human Resources to save as many jobs as they can during the pandemic, defensiveness strategy helped organizations as many people selected early retirement to augment the vast number of layoffs due to COVID-19.

As the post-pandemic recovery unfolds, futurity strategy promotes the process of knowledge application by providing a series of guidelines for companies, aiming at tracking trends, conducting "what-if" analysis, allocating capabilities, and adapting actions accordingly.

These proposed linkages can be illustrated in the following figure.

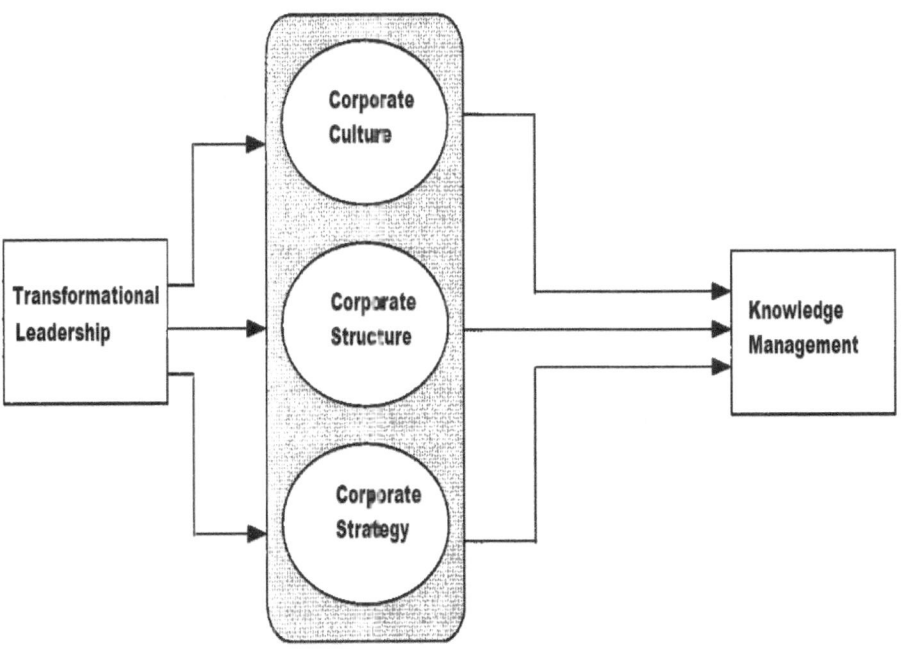

Chapter Summary

In this chapter, we offer several implications for practice as we work through the pandemic of COVID-19. We highlight the vital importance of transformational leadership and the three tenets of culture, structure, and technology, as catalysts in affecting knowledge management both today and in preparation for the post-pandemic recovery.

We reveal that transformational leadership has significant effects on organizational factors as leaders navigate an iterative process of sustaining business when many organizations are in survival mode. Leadership and strategy initiatives have monitored and steered organizations through this turbulent time.

We highlight the vital importance of transformational leadership to stimulate a culture of learning as many followers are working remotely, building upon the collaboration involvement of employees, customers, and clients, and providing a trusting environment for both leaders and their remote workers. The flattened workforce scaled down to remote meetings, that was once in the office is now working remotely impacting the organizational structure now and in the future. To augment this new challenge, there is a vast need for executives to improve strategic initiatives.

Chapter 3: Post-Pandemic Recovery with Technology and Knowledge Management

Bridging the gap of academic journals and crossover literature has been the focal point of executive prowess. Executives want quick facts, *how-to* articles like the Harvard Business Review and Forbes and the academic research have not reached them enough.

In this chapter, we attempt to blend scholarly concepts with real world application to ensure a crisp difference in what really works, what should be read, and most importantly, what should be applied in the workplace during the post-pandemic recovery. Blending transformational leadership and technology management are two natural consequences of leadership action to enhance the post-pandemic recovery. We suggest the use of a pivotal technology change along with inculcated change efforts formulated by using the transformational leadership model to enhance communication and followership. We introduce a **TRANSFORMATIONAL TECHNOLOGY LEADERSHIP** approach to master the art of the post-pandemic recovery.

Many executives are focusing on leadership, knowledge management, and information technology. Here are some of the ideas that we gathered from 78 executives leading during the pandemic. Since our research is based upon Transformational Leadership, this was our primary leadership model. With transformational leadership, we found that the post-pandemic recovery requires effective technological infrastructure that is developed to monitor and sustain competitive advantage. When the pandemic first began, March 2020, executives strived to meet the customer needs while maintaining employee satisfaction levels, along with preserving their publicly traded stockholder equity.

Strategic objectives are constantly being tweaked to include supplier support and vendor relationships as the world manages the pandemic. The primary function of knowledge management is to restructure unclear and vague situations into a set of organizationally resolvable problems. Solutions are key to a firm's success as the pandemic evolves. Knowledge management is implemented and formulated to efficiently deploy the organizational capabilities and interact with the global environment.

Executives are also setting goals that are not only realistic and specific but also are flexible, leaving room for change and adaptation. Transformational leaders are posited to engage in the facilitation of achieving more sustainable changes in organizations. We propose the following questions:

1. How does transformational leadership impact knowledge management in the post-pandemic world?
2. How can we use information technology to mediate the relationship between transformational leadership and knowledge management?

Theoretical Insights

To best describe the actions necessary to handle to tumultuous post-pandemic, we emphasize the importance of a concept called *The Knowledge-Based View*. Our reasoning is that more so today then pre-pandemic times, organizations exist as social communities designed to enhance competitive advantage by utilizing and creating new ideas and knowledge. Knowledge creation and utilization manifest themselves as constructs of the knowledge-based view. [1] [2]

Executives taking a knowledge-based view of their organization begin to draw upon various organizational factors that mediate the relationship between knowledge management and transformational leadership. The knowledge-based view of an organization underpins the various organizational factors that link transformational leadership and knowledge management together to better perform in a post-pandemic world. The post-pandemic recovery places transformational leaders in a position to develop technological infrastructures quickly and effectively and disseminate this knowledge and use thoroughly and thoughtfully. The question arises: **How do we manage knowledge when everyone is remotely engaged?** This question resides in not only the C-Suite but through all levels or the organization.

Thus, this chapter attempts to advance the post-pandemic approach of transformational leadership and knowledge management.

The Knowledge Based View

The knowledge-based view emerges and highlights that the firm's capabilities to utilize and create knowledge are most crucial for sustainable competitive advantage. The new knowledge created from the pandemic concurrent remote work has eluded that functionality is existential to performance. In fact, a firm's capabilities allow it to leverage knowledge in a more efficient manner using technological platforms that once existed as a past time as opposed to a necessary medium for success. Zoom, Microsoft Teams, and WebEx are a few platforms that are usefu for electronic meetings.

The knowledge-based view focuses on embedding knowledge in organizational members, attempting to uncover tacit knowledge embedded within employees because tacit knowledge may be a more important source of competitive advantage then explicit knowledge. [3] [4] [5]

Many people find themselves at home sitting behind a computer in meetings and as this process has now become the norm and technology has enhanced this platform. The rebirth of information technology has affected competitive advantage through enabling knowledge within companies to present itself as an internal resource. Working remotely has been controlled by organizations effectively and continues to do so. Effectiveness and efficiency, while still in survival mode, are tantamount to an organization's survival in the post-pandemic recovery.

The post-pandemic has led to patterns of change efforts that must constantly be tweaked in real time as organizations manifest the recovery. Information technology, while always important, has embraced organizations in an attempt to survive. Information technology is adaptable for every organization and each individual, but people are apprehensive and training and development along with strong communication is key to survival. In order to have a chance for survival in a concurrent pandemic world, we found that organizations that embrace technology survive.

Employee behavior, becoming more of an issue of accountability, has become an elusive target as many people are not sitting by the computer all day and yet the perception is that human resources are available 24-hours a day, seven days a week. The nine-to-five work week is becoming extinct, yet, the super employee is become the elite contender. The question is:

Can a person manage a work life balance in the post-pandemic world?

Except for an occasional time-lapse for both evaluation and application, technological infrastructures have adapted accordingly and there is a considerable alignment between the knowledge-based view of the firm and information technology. There is a strong application that executives may miss because the academic literature does not advertise the benefits or research and findings in this area. However, the savvy executive will improve communication among remote workers adequately and efficiently as many academic notions are common-sense applications. For example, remote worker knowledge acquired through learning from others and information technology is a strategic factor for competitive advantage in the post-COVID era that delivers a broad spectrum of reliability if used appropriately. Thus, developing a personal space for communication and presentation is an effective used of time and resources because information technology when used as an internal resource can positively influence competitive advantage through developing platforms for remote workers.

We found that a vital role in effectively managing the post-pandemic recovery is the use of transformational leadership. By using transformational leadership to lead technological changes, executives, and followers' row in the same direction to better manage organizational knowledge, its dissemination, and most importantly, its application.

The Vital Role of the Transformational Leader

Executives, focusing on consultants, academics, and technological experts, are taking a serious look at all leadership ideas and suggestions today with the plethora of options available to them. Some are focusing on transformational leadership while others select different leadership applications or simply create their own leadership philosophy. We found that prior researchers show the crucial role of transformational leadership in facilitating the knowledge acquisition process and ensuring competitive advantage in a hypercompetitive work environment. [6] [7] Thus, if scholars agree that transformational leadership improves knowledge integration through enhancing knowledge sharing, then executives should climb on board and implement a strong communication system that includes technology, knowledge management, and transformational leadership. [8] Why should executives agree to this leadership implication? The reason being is that "More scholars found that transformational leadership builds a climate that inspires followers to share knowledge in a productive and prosperous manner," [9] [10] and, in order to master the art of success in a post-pandemic world, both scholars and executives must unite in solidarity.

The executives we met with felt that sixty percent of their time was based upon following up and tweaking strategic initiatives and this increased due to the pandemic and became more prevalent around March 2020. Executives spend a great deal of time conceptualizing strategic endeavors. Scholars affirm that conceptualizing in the strategic role, transformational leaders enhance decision-making when information technology implementation occurs at the right time and place. [11] This is nothing new, however. Dan Isenberg in a Harvard Business Review article titled "How Senior Manager's Think," in November 1984 found that executives are much more dynamic as people assume them to be.

> Most successful senior managers do not closely follow the classical rational model of first clarifying goals, assessing the situation, formulating options, estimating likelihoods of success, making their decision, and only then taking action to implement the decision. Nor do top managers select one problem at a time to solve, as the rational model implies. Instead of having precise goals and objectives, successful senior executives have general overriding concerns and think more often about how to do things than about what is being accomplished. (Daniel Isenberg)

Thus, we found that transformational leaders raise the levels of awareness of the importance of technology and empower people to improve their use of information technology when implementing strategic initiatives within organizations.

Informational technology is one of most prominent organizational resources that facilitates organizational communication and improves the search for knowledge. We found that transformational leaders enhance effectiveness when they blend technological communication to enhance their leadership role. [12] There is a significant correlation between transformational leadership and perceived usefulness of the information technology within organizations. [13] In particular, transformational leaders enable employees to analyze problems and challenge followers to be more innovative.

The knowledge-based view in the post-COVID world is vibrant and, in some cases, used on a real-time basis with changes to documents live as information is shared, updated, and read in meetings.

There are limitations to the knowledge-based view in that security could be breached and hackers can conduct what is known as "Zoom Bombing," which indicates that hackers join sessions inadvertently. Home invasion of home-based internet connections is also a potential problem when conducting meetings in cyberspace.

Many organizations managed to capitalize on information technology and continue to thrive in the post-pandemic recovery. The capability of organizations to integrate the employee's specialized knowledge into products and services can largely generate competitive advantage for them. Hence, executives found that the information technology that reflects an internal resource that is used to manage knowledge and create competitive advantage could help their organization thrive in the post-pandemic world.

Chapter Summary

This chapter advances the current literature on transformational leadership by offering novel insights into how executives can have a sizable impact on information technology and knowledge management now as they prepare for the post-pandemic. As executives enable information technology and knowledge management, their organization may not only survive but also thrive. Thus, grasping upon these three tenets is essential in the post-pandemic recovery.

The following figure provides a snapshot of how transformational leadership, information technology and knowledge management are linked.

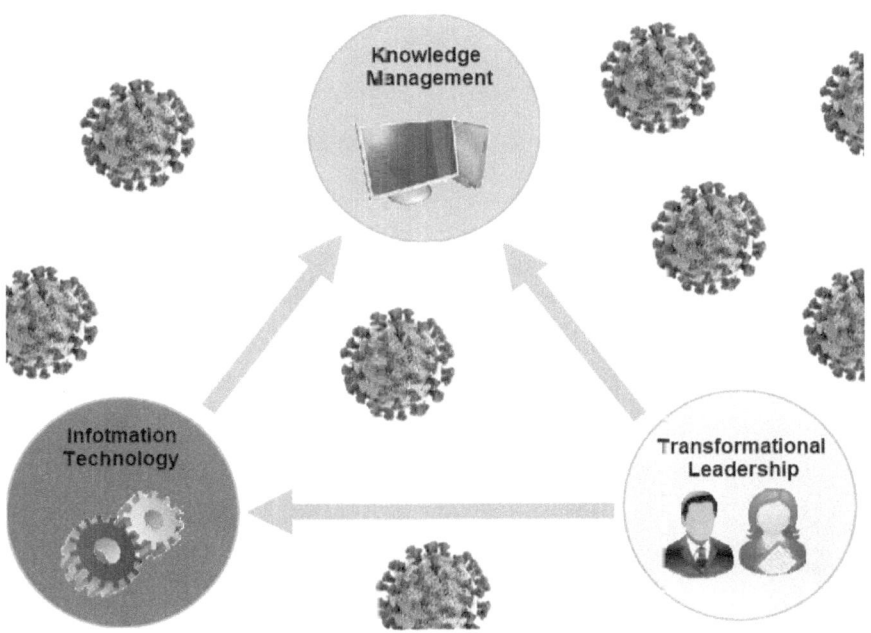

Executives agree that transformational leadership, information technology, and knowledge management have played a significant role in recovery plans during the pandemic. This is not the sole concern for the post-pandemic recovery, however, because there are, and continue to be, many facets of the pandemic that relate to transformations of many kinds and not only these three tenets.

We found that transformational leaders are change agents who manage information technology to develop knowledge management. Ergo, embracing this new model of executive leadership, among the many other concerns of the post-pandemic recovery, will help organizations prosper.

Chapter 4: Post-Pandemic Recovery Using Human Resource Technology

Knowledge management has become a focal point of executive span of control but has not been associated with Human Resource technology enough to make it an integral part of business success. Being on the forefront of knowledge is an importance competence as organizations across the globe recovery from COVID-19.

Knowledge management processes are enhanced when coupled with technology to organize existing information. Technology plays a crucial role in creating, retrieving, storing, and applying organizational knowledge.

Apurva Anand and Singh say that technology embraces "intelligent searching, categorization and accessing of data from disparate databases, E-mail, texting, and files." [1] Many organizations focus on individuals as the major source of knowledge and show how they can affect the sharing, storage, transfer, and application of knowledge within organizations. Shared knowledge and memory are central to the effectiveness of knowledge management.

Human resource technology enables organizations to build knowledge-based systems that can create and implement innovations timely as they operate and compete in global markets. Knowledge-based systems embraces Human Resource technology to store, retrieve, and keep track of not only employee records and accomplishments but also employee health concerns and, in the post-pandemic, the tracking of the COVID19 health and vaccination status of each employee. This prevents the spread of COVID-19 and the far-reaching variants to come. Creating a conducive organizational climate that fosters knowledge management is key to post-pandemic recovery.

Unshared knowledge is like lettuce in the refrigerator---if shared, everyone enjoys it, if not shared and left alone, it wilts and does not have any use. As the pandemic unfolded, human resources expanded its reach to include safety, security, training, remote-hiring, and, in some cases, remote firing. Data on the extent and reach of human resources is an ever-changing event which is continuously improving, and this will continue in the post-pandemic recovery.

Managing Knowledge and Human Resource Technology

Knowledge resides in various areas of organizations, and how it is tracked, disseminated, and made available to the public is an important role when enhancing organizational functions. Where knowledge lies and how it can be captured, utilized, and used when it comes to decision-making is a strong concern in the post-pandemic.

Jay Barney, an author and scholar in the area of management at Yale University, presented executives with the knowledge-based view of the firm and a slew of internal resources that provided a direct vision for the organization. The knowledge-based view focused on embedding knowledge in each member of the organization. This approach uncovers knowledge embedded among employees and can be an important factor for competitive advantage. Executives, therefore, embrace various internal resources affecting competitive advantage through enabling knowledge within organizations to prosper.

Human resource technology is an internal resource that increasingly facilitates the business processes and improves the search for information and knowledge in and around the organization. For example, Human Resource Information

System (HRIS) software enables companies to overcome space constraints in communications and promotes the depth and range of knowledge access. HRIS software can also be employed to enhance the conversations and knowledge exchanges between organizational members.

Three prominent scholars that are well known in the Academy of Management, one of the largest leadership and management organizations in the world, by the names of Andrew Gold, Arvind Malhotra, and Albert Segars argue that this knowledge shared through technology could positively contribute to knowledge integration. Knowledge integration refers to the process of merging two or more originally unrelated knowledge structures into a single structure to improve culture, systems, and the delivery of products and services. Executives apply HRIS software to develop and disseminate information throughout the organization which improves the search for information in order to adapt to today's uncertain business environment.

Human Capital Management (HCM) software is another important resource for strategic planning for knowledge integration. Robert Grant highlights knowledge integration as a major reason for the existence of an organization. [4] This software enhances learning and sharing information by providing access to the most accurate information and knowledge. HCM software also stimulates new knowledge generation, through transferring knowledge to other organizational members and departments. Knowledge sharing in and of itself can in turn develop a more innovative climate and facilitate knowledge creation. HCM software can, therefore, play a crucial role in improving knowledge creation and transference of data. Executives can use HCM software to develop an effective learning culture that disseminates knowledge throughout the organization.

Human Resource Management System (HRMS) software can also be used by executives to facilitate knowledge creation processes through providing the essential infrastructure to store and retrieve organizational knowledge. HRMS software encourages executives to embark on technological facilities to provide new solutions for solving organizational problems and transferring individual knowledge to other members and departments. The right Infrastructure can improve knowledge capturing, create a better system of storing and retrieving knowledge, and accumulating knowledge to achieve organizational goals and objectives.

Chapter Summary

This chapter advances the current literature on Human Resource technology and knowledge management by offering novel insights into how to incorporate Human Resource technology to enhance the post-pandemic recovery. Updating, communicating, and disseminating information leads to better knowledge management post the Covid-19 pandemic. This chapter also portrays a more detailed picture of the effects of Human Resource technology on knowledge management in the post-Covid-19 world.

Executives can apply Human Resource technology in their decision-making processes in order to investigate various alternatives, possible solutions to problems, and generate options to augment the ever-changing threat of the Corona Virus. Thus, success in today's global business environment can be more effective when Human Resource technology is effectively applied and widely used to achieve a higher degree of competitive advantage.

Executives can implement HR technology through employing information technology professionals to help them allocate more budgetary resources to share and utilize knowledge within organizations. Knowledge management performance at all levels of the organization is positively associated with using Human Resource technology and by using both, in tandem, leaders can enhance the changing complexity of strategic decision-making.

Chapter 5: Post-Pandemic Recovery Strategy Formulation

*I*n this chapter, we posit that knowledge management can play a crucial role in preparing an organization for the post-pandemic recovery. Strategic planning, promoting growth, possessing technology savvy, and managing retrenchment during the post-pandemic recovery are essential skills of the executive. Executives have so much on their plate in the post pandemic recovery. What worked in the nineties will not work today because people are as important as organizational structure. You may ask Why? Ron Willingham answers:

"Organizations don't produce; people do! When organizational structure itself becomes more important that the people within it, trouble inevitably lies ahead."

Source: *(*Willingham, 1997, The People Principle: A Revolutionary Redefinition of Leadership, St. Martin's Press, New York, p. 24)

We found vital importance of two strategic aspects: One, a thorough and continuous analysis, and the second being proactive implementation and tweaking. Both can be done using the collection, dissemination, and management of organizational knowledge. Organizational strategy is tantamount and will continue to be important in the post-pandemic era. The Mostafa Sayyadi research team conducted research in a large consulting firm in the Middle East and North America Region. The United States' trade and investment relations with the countries of the Middle East and North Africa (MENA) have considerable potential value in terms of both U.S. commercial and foreign policy interests according to the Office of the United States Trade Representatives, and executive office of the President of the United States.

The team asked executives what the post-pandemic world would look like not only in that region but what the global environment would be like in the post-pandemic recovery.

We found that knowledge management and corporate strategy have more attention, in the C-Suite, since the post-pandemic, due to the large platforms of remote workers.

Executives realize the need to develop an analysis strategy to provide new and innovative solutions for organizational problems. Executives can develop an effective analysis strategy through taking the following actions:

1. Focus on the effective coordination among different functional areas.
2. Use various information systems (such as Executive Support Systems (ESS), Management Information Systems (MIS), Decision Support Systems (DSS), Knowledge Management Systems (KMS), Transaction Processing Systems (TPS), Office Automation Systems (OAS), and Group Decision Support Systems (GDSS)) to support decision making.
3. Use various business-planning methods (such as Cost–Benefit Analysis, Risk Assessment, Environmental

Assessment, Program Evaluation, Participatory Methods, and 360-Degree Performance Evaluation).

4. Use control systems (such as Linear Control Systems, Non-linear Control Systems, Analog or Continuous Systems, Digital or Discrete Systems, Single Input Single Output Systems, Multiple Input Multiple Output Systems, Lumped Parameter Systems, Distributed Parameter Systems, and Group Decision Making Systems).

5. Use various cost control methods (such as Process Costing, Job Costing, Direct Costing, and Cost-Benefit Analysis) for effectively monitoring of company performance.

6. Use various management performance methods (such as Key Performance Indicators (KPIs) and Metrics, Balanced Scorecards, Personal Development Plans (PDP), and Career Succession Planning) to ensure that you cover the employee knowledge and expertise.

7. Use various manpower planning and performance appraisal methods (such as Management by Objectives (MBO), 360-Degree Feedback, Assessment Centre Method, Behaviourally Anchored Rating Scale (BARS), Psychological Appraisals, Human-Resource (Cost) Accounting Method, Leadership Performance Index

Survey, Thomas' Workplace Personality Assessment, and the Plan Do Study Act) for senior managers.

While more work is necessary to determine the benefits of anonymity on idea generation and evaluation (Jessup, Connoly, and Galegher), a proactiveness strategy takes an optimal approach to search for better positions in the business environment. [1] [2] [3] [4] [5] Impersonality may reduce inhibitions, and this may have a significant effect on group problem solving, and group decision making is becoming more applicable today as we survive the pandemic and prepare for the post-pandemic recovery.

Organizational Developer practitioners are taking the following actions to engage in the facilitation of pro-activeness strategy:

1. Actively search businesses that can be acquired.
2. Actively introduce new brands or products in the market.
3. Track significant and general trends in the market.
4. Focus on basic research to provide organizations with a competitive edge for the future.
5. Regularly modify the manufacturing and service technology.

6. Eliminate those operations that are no longer profitable in the later stages of their life cycles. Discontinue if necessary.
7. Focus on key indicators of operations forecasted (such as customer satisfaction, internal process quality, employee satisfaction, financial performance index, and capital asset pricing models).

A Large Consulting Firm Perspective on the Post-Pandemic Recovery

Sayyadi and team sent out an online survey to informants which was conducted to acquire empirical data. Company size was a crucial criterion for this research. A large organization was defined as the company with 400 or more employees and that was a criterion in which the researchers selected from a large pool of employees. The Sayyadi team of researchers targeted managers and the internal Organizational Development area of a large consulting firm. The Strategic Orientation Questionnaire was adopted to measure two aspects of corporate strategy. The survey included both analysis strategy and pro-active strategy. A sample of the items in the survey are:

- Our company effectively uses the data provided by control systems and management information systems.

- Our company actively looks for new opportunities in today's global market environment.

The knowledge management construct measured knowledge management practices in this organization. The sample items of this survey include:

- Our company has effective mechanisms to make sure every employee understands customer and shareholder needs.
- Our company is involved in cooperative and collaborative arrangements with other companies (excluding contract Research and Development).

After conducting data analysis, the results suggested an acceptable degree of reliability (Cronbach Alpha 83.725) for the two constructs of this research. Consistent with predictions, results showed that corporate strategy had a sizable and positive impact on knowledge management development.

This research, even on a small scale, represents a step forward in specifying corporate strategy as a key factor in cultivating an effective influence on knowledge management performance. We found that corporate strategy had an impact on knowledge management. Thus, we posit that managing knowledge in the post-pandemic recovery will be beneficial to organizations.

Chapter Summary

Corporate strategy can be enhanced by managing organizational knowledge. We emphasize the importance of a knowledge-based strategy for the post-pandemic recovery. It is evident that corporate strategy can assist organizational knowledge management. We found that strategy determines how companies manage their organizational knowledge assets to survive the pandemic. Ergo, knowledge is equity.

We based our research on Dan Isenberg's findings that indicated that senior managers tend to think about two kinds of problems: ***how to create effective organizational processes and how to deal with one or two overriding concerns, or very general goals.*** These two domains of thought underlie the two critical activities that John P. Kotter found general managers engaged in: developing and maintaining an extensive interpersonal network and formulating an agenda. Dan Isenberg, captured this in a Harvard Business Review article, titled, "How Senior Manager's Think," in November 1984. We feel that how executives think is more pertinent and applicable today as we navigate the post-pandemic recovery.

Organizational Development scholars can have a direct impact on corporate strategy as organizations prepare for the post-pandemic recovery. Scholars should focus on helping executives create knowledge-based strategic initiatives through robust empirical research.

Chapter 6: Transformational Leadership Development in a Post-pandemic World

*W*hen we decided to write this book, the world was in turmoil. COVID19 spread across continents leaving not a stone unturned. We asked executives how they feel, most importantly, how they wanted to feel. The response was overwhelming. Most responses hovered around the fact that the future was uncertain and unprecedented times are in their near future. This is what gave us the impetus to study the effects of transformational leadership upon organizational performance.

Jim Clawson, in his book "Fundamentals of Level Three Leadership," published by Business Expert Press, argues that:

> Many people malign large corporations. And there is much that needs improving in them, not the least of which is the proportional divide between extractors and contributors…. Sustainable trade makes friends of otherwise distrustful enemies. Short-term extraction with unbalanced benefits is not a viable long-term strategy. Mutual benefit and related trust over time brings businesspeople to each other's tables……If those dreams are based on unbalanced extraction or control, the sustainability erodes…. Businesspeople want stable markets, stable political environments, sable exchange rates, and stability around the table. (2021, Page 124, How to Become and Effective Executive)

We found that transformational leadership has influenced organizational performance in many ways. As a significant indicator of organizational performance, the word transformation alone has resonated in the C-Suite.

Companies that claim to be "transforming" seem to be everywhere. But when you look more deeply into whether those organizations are truly redefining what they are and what they do, stories of successful change efforts are exceptionally rare. In a study of S&P 500 and Global 500 firms, our team found that those leading the most successful transformations, creating new offerings and business models to push into new growth markets, share common characteristics and strategies. ____ (Scott Anthony and Evan Schwartz, 2017, What the Best Transformational Leaders Do, Harvard Business Review)

We feel that executives that act as transformational leaders affect organizational outcomes in positive ways. In particular, we raise a vital question as to how managers can successfully contribute to performance during turbulent times such as the post-pandemic recovery. We highlight the potential benefits of applying transformational leadership. However, we admit possible blind spots. Scholars noticed blind spots to be a CEO disease because it is not easy for leaders to identify their strengths and gaps on their own (p. 134, Primal Leadership, Dan Goleman, Dick Boyatzis, and Ann McKee, Harvard Business School Press, Boston, Massachusetts). Thus, we hope to advance the literature to include a possible correlation between transformational leadership within organizations and how that impacts organizational performance.

A Brief Look at Transformational leadership and Company Performance

First and foremost, there are four dimensions that have been determined for transformational leadership, including *idealized influence, inspirational motivation, intellectual stimulation, and individualized consideration.* [1]

Prior research indicates many applications of Transformational leadership and two dimensions are captured below.

Idealized influence. Transformational leaders can

positively enhance collaboration through idealized influence by developing relationships with subordinates throughout the organization. Collaboration is highly facilitated by diminishing isolation and providing opportunities for further dialogue. [2] It can build a climate of openness for employees to link their individual-interests to collective-interests. [3] A transformational leader also shows concern through individualized consideration by focusing on identifying employees' individual needs within companies. It can be argued that this concern for employees' individual needs can in turn contribute to their organizational commitment and inspire them to put extra effort into their jobs, which leads to improved quality of products and services, increased customer satisfaction, and eventually, extra effort by employees may promote the degree of return on assets, sales, and return on equity.

Inspirational motivation. Transformational leadership also highlights the vital importance of employee attitudes in accomplishing the goals and objectives of the organization. In this way, the inspirational motivation aspect of transformational leadership can inspire human capital through setting highly desired expectations. [4] A higher level of expectation can motivate human assets to enhance their productivity, and in some cases, this may decrease organizational costs of training and development in this area.

Several researchers show that the transformational leadership enhances various financial and non-financial indicators of organizational performance. [5] [6] [7] [8] [9] [10] [11] [12] [13] These financial and non-financial indicators include improving the price of stock, improving response to environmental changes, improving the quality of products, and improving customer satisfaction and developing opportunities for learning and growth. Therefore, it can be argued that performance at the organizational level is a product of transformational leadership.

The MENA Region Findings

The Sayyadi team of researchers summarize findings of an empirical investigation within large and medium-sized organizations. Based on a random sample, the population of this study is comprised of organizations across the Middle East and North Africa (MENA) region. The organizations represent a wide variety of industries including manufacturing, service providers, as well as public, and private organizations.

With transformational leadership being one of many prominent leadership models and theories used in the post pandemic recovery, we attempt to add to the extant literature at a crucial time as the world recovers from an unprecedented pandemic.

Our goal is to expand the extant literature. We do this

by conducting an empirical study of business professionals to develop a research framework that expands the current literature in the area of transformational leadership. Our research team constrained this study to one geographical area (i.e. the MENA region). We used a random sampling technique as a set of data that provided a clear picture of the current situation of large and medium-sized organizations operating in the MENA region.

This empirical study was designed to ask participants to provide their perceptions on two latent variables (i.e. transformational leadership and organizational performance). We collected data from both leaders and followers. Our reasoning for this research design is that previous studies indicate that followers and line managers may have a wider perspective of organizational processes. [14] We felt that apart from the critical role of senior leaders as strategic decision makers, middle managers may also have a wider perspective of the effectiveness of the organizational process. [15] [16] We felt that senior leaders, middle managers, line managers and employees, are qualified to provide their perceptions on the research variables of this research.

Our research design included an online survey sent to informants to acquire empirical data on the largest scale possible for the organizations investigated. We followed the work of Rohit Deshpande, who argued that a survey method measures organizational characteristics by examining informant's perceptions. [17] Company size was also a crucial criterion for this study, and we used a random sample which was sufficient to represent the selected population. Accordingly, large, and medium-sized organizations have been defined as the companies with 100 or more employees and that was a criterion in which we based our research. The companies selected, were not limited to a specific industry and, therefore, are broadly representative of businesses perspectives. As mentioned earlier, the participants were selected and were solicited from a large pool of both followers and leaders in large and medium-sized companies.

The Multifactor Leadership Questionnaire (MLQ) was adopted to measure four aspects of transformational leadership, including idealized influence, inspirational motivation, intellectual stimulation, and individual consideration. This questionnaire was designed and validated by Bernard Bass and Bruce Avolio. [18] The sample items in this category included:

- In our company, leaders enable others to think about old problems in new ways.
- In our company, leaders help others to develop.

We also measured items for organizational performance relied upon financial and non-financial performance. The sample items in this category included:

- Our company has been excellent in meeting its goals over the past five years.
- Our company has been able to acquire the financial resources it needs over the past five years.

The research design included the following demographics:

- 306 chief executive officers participated n the survey
- 402 chief executive officers recommended other suitable leaders or employees to part cipate on their behalf.

Subsequently, these leaders and employees were surveyed by an email that was sent to them with a consent form and a link to an online questionnaire offering a secure site on which to take the survey. A tota of 708 online questionnaires were sent to participating companies.

Of the 708 surveys sent out to the participants, a total of 643 questionnaires were returned, representing an overall response rate of 90.81 percent. Among these returned responses, 21 surveys were not useable or were considered incomplete and tabled as unusable for this industry research. This resulted in 622 responses (i.e., 96.73 percent of the returned surveys) from 457 large and medium-sized organizations. The sample characteristics have been presented in the following tables:

Table 1: Average Age

Average Age	Frequency	Percent
Age range 20 and 25 years old	76	12.21
Age range 26 and 30 years old	92	14.79
Age range 31 and 35 years old	131	21.06
Age range 36 and 40 years old	123	19.77
Age range 41 and 45 years old	136	21.86
Older than 45 years old	64	10.28

* N = 622

Table 2: Job Rank

Job Rank	Frequency	Percent
Employees	248	39.87
Managers	374	60.12

* N = 622

Table 3: Gender

Job Rank	Frequency	Percent
Female	191	30.71
Male	431	69.29

* N = 622

Table 4: Years of Service

Years of Service	Frequency	Percent
Less than 1 year	103	16.55
Between 1and 10 years	247	39.71
Between 11 and 20 years	149	23.95
More than 20 years	123	19.77

* N = 622

Table 5: Organization Size

Organization Size	Frequency	Percent
Between 100 and 200 employees	211	46.17
Between 201 and 300 employees	78	17.06
More than 300 employees	168	36.76

* N = 457

Table 6: Organization Type

Organization Type	Frequency	Percent
Public	124	27.13
Private	333	72.86

* N = 457

Findings

Our study had a two-pronged effect. One, can we discover the extend of transformational leadership practice in a particular region of the world and with the array of organizations found in this region? Secondly, once determined, does level and extent of transformational leadership have an impact on organizational performance?

Consistent with our predictions that transformational leadership impacts organizational performance, results showed that transformational leadership had a sizable and positive impact on organizational performance in large and medium-sized companies in the MENA region. Thus, the results of this empirical study supported this theoretical linkage.

How Can Executives Use These Findings?

This empirical study suggests new insights to identify transformational leadership as a primary driver, which influences organizational performance. More broadly, it can be argued that when executives decide that performance becomes increasingly valuable as a competitive advantage, then we predict that transformational leadership manifests as a catalyst to increase firm performance. It follows that improving organizational resources requires, as a strong predictor, the development of transformational leadership within organizations. Thus, we suggest that a firm's ability to enhance organizational performance can be effective by the transformational leadership model adopted by managers within organizations. In particular, this research points out the vital importance of transformational leadership in developing higher performing organizations in the post-pandemic recovery.

How Can Scholars Use These Findings?

This research provides evidence that transformational leadership when coupled with organizational performance offers improvement not only in employee satisfaction and motivation but also in the profitability of the organization. It extends these lines of study by uncovering the argument that managers who embrace transformational leadership style have a positive impact on organizational performance. The findings of this study fill a gap in the literature by portraying a more detailed picture of the effects of this leadership style on organizational performance.

Limitations

First and foremost, we are placing financial

performance in a category of its own in that we may assume that financial stability may have many factors. Given that we measured transformational leadership within these organizations, we feel that it is safe to say there is a linkage. On the other hand, if we found that transformational leadership is non-existent, then the financial linkage would be weak. Second, we selected the MENA region because of our contacts and viability to approach executives. In many cases, executives are too busy and disregard solicitation of leadership inquiry, and more importantly, financial inquiry. Thus, with this in mind, a willingness to share our data got us not only in the door to conduct research but we were also welcomed. We look at this a "Hawthorne Effect." Since we showed an interest and addressed the region with our empirical interest, the executives felt compelled to get others onboard to fill out the surveys. Although, still a limitation, we appreciated the encouragement to ask pertinent people to fill out our surveys. For example, four hundred and two chief executive officers recommended other suitable leaders or employees to participate on their behalf. While this benefited our research, it also become somewhat contrived because scholars may feel that these suitable leaders may have been handpicked.

Future Research Directions

This chapter provides not only an expansion of the literature on transformational leadership and organizational performance but also develops a new research design that can be replicated, expanded, and extrapolated.

We recommend that future studies develop a more comprehensive understanding of the relationship between transformational leadership and organizational performance through measuring these linkages within specific industries. A more global perspective is desirable and future empirical studies can introduce more objective measurements addressing the international management perspective to examine the research variables proposed here. For example, Richard Allen and Ralph Kilmann suggest that researchers also use absolute financial numbers to measure firms' performance in terms of profits and sales. [19] Sabine Bischoff, Gergana Vladova, and Sabina Jeschke also suggest that the intangible-asset-monitor method should be used to measure company performance through evaluating various indicators such as turnover rate, the proportion of support staff, and value added per employee and expert. [20]

Finally, linking organizational resources such as remote team functionality and satisfaction that may have relevance in the post-pandemic recovery could also spur new insights.

Future research could explore how organizational climate, remote work, electronic communication software, and employee satisfaction is influenced when working remotely. How these factors are influenced by transformational leadership to improve organizational performance would be a fruitful inquiry.

Chapter Summary

Consistent with our predictions, our results showed that transformational leadership had a sizable and positive impact on organizational performance in large and medium-sized companies in the MENA region. Results of this empirical study supported our theoretical linkage that resources, not only human resources, but resources in general, when coupled with transformational leadership may strongly contribute to organizational performance.

Chapter 7: Transformational Leadership, Knowledge Management and Company Performance

*I*n chapter six, we measured transformational leadership and organizational performance and we found that they correlate well together. We feel that adding the concept of knowledge management can further the post-pandemic recovery because there are new advances in technology and business concerns are continuously developing.

This chapter highlights some theoretical findings indicative of our proposed model of Transformational Leadership, Organizational Performance, and Knowledge management, revisits the marriage we posited for transformational leadership and organizational performance, then introduces our additional component, knowledge management.

Knowledge Management

In examining the relationship between social capital and knowledge management, Polanyi (1966) argues that knowledge emerges in interactions and therefore it is a necessary precursor to create knowledge. The key for executives in the post-pandemic is to build a structure of strong relationships and more participation. [1] Following this approach, scholars argue that social capital is an important facilitator of knowledge [2] [3] [4] [5] and these scholars describe a firm "*as a social community specializing in the speed and efficiency in the creation and transfer of knowledge*." [6] We found, in our executive trainings, that during the pandemic, there was a need for survival with little light at the end of the tunnel. However, as the pandemic began to subside, strategic initiatives manifested strong relationships from electronic meetings and the added resilience that led a worldwide recovery.

How do we communicate electronically in meetings? What happens after the meeting? Is there a follow-up meeting? We found that electronic meetings are stressful enough and time consuming. There are virtually no follow up meetings and whatever happens in the meeting stays in that meeting. Thus, tacit knowledge is unused, untapped, and unappreciated in electronic meetings. Nonaka and Takeuchi (1995) propose socialization as an essential requirement of knowledge creation by which knowledge can be created through sharing tacit knowledge among people. [7] Therefore, it is reasonable to argue that trust-based relationships, as a construct of social capital, inspire organizational members to share their tacit knowledge to generate new ideas within companies. Executives are encouraged to create follow-up meetings and further communication based upon the dialogue during meetings. Ergo, social capital needs to be nurtured in the post-pandemic to ensure improved knowledge sharing.

In some organizations, an in-group and out-group becomes more transparent in electronic meetings. People in the outgroup may speak out of turn or become too opinionated while the ingroup participants are called upon and revered. Executives should be sensitive to not praise one person without acknowledging others and the same with reprimanding or speaking negatively about a person, a project, or an opinion. Our reasoning for this position is based upon the fact that social networks are a central construct of social capital, comprised of communities of practice defined as "relatively tight-knit groups of people who know each other and work together directly." [3] When approached positively, electronic meetings can foster strong camaraderie.

Gordon (2002) postulates that communities of practice frequently solve technical problems and that members share their ideas and knowledge together. [9] This frequent contact and willingness to share existing practice and knowledge to solve technical problems, can in turn enhance a shared understanding among members. Therefore, shared understanding is welcomed because we found that trust-based relationships and social networks can positively contribute to knowledge and facilitate knowledge management within organizations. A key survival mechanism for the post-pandemic recovery is trust-based relationships.

Transformational Leadership

In addition to the knowledge management construct mentioned above, transformational leadership instills major changes at the organizational level through an attempt to change attitudes and assumptions at the individual level. This theory of leadership highlights the importance of employees' attitudes and values in achieving organizational goals and describes effective organizational change as a product of developing relationships with subordinates.

Transformational leadership fosters human assets and then moves them beyond self-interests by aligning the individuals' interests with the collective interests of the organization. [10] Transformational leaders aggregate human capital into social capital to implement changes at the organizational level and provide valuable resources for the organization. This leadership theory, based on the executives we surveyed, has been the focal point of the post-pandemic recovery.

As mentioned in the section above, social capital is a precursor to knowledge management and, in addition to this construct, a strong alignment can be found between transformational leadership theory and social capital theory. In fact, transformational leadership theory is associated with social networks and trust-based relationships. For example, Pemberton, Mavin and Stalker's (2007: 67) found that communities of practice consist of like-minded people whose interconnectedness require a form of leadership in which "the freedom to explore new ideas and set its own agenda, free from the shackles of organizational missives, has been achieved by the commitment of its members and facilitated by a coordinator acting as a transformational leader for the purposes of organizing meetings." [11] Thus, transformational leadership theory practiced today in the post-pandemic is a key ingredient of social networking.

Transformational leadership facilitates knowledge sharing through applying intellectual stimulation that enhances knowledge sharing among human assets. Similarly, Braga (2002: 16) maintains that transformational leaders are effective networkers who provide "a flow of ideas, questions, and assumptions that are necessary to stimulate productive communication" within organizations. [12] Transformational leaders become role models [12] who are trusted, admired and respected by followers. [13] Therefore, transformational leaders inspire their followers to develop trust-based relationships among them and transformational leadership theory is strongly related to the social capital theory.

Transformational Leadership and Knowledge Management

Executives, worldwide, have found that idealized influence is about generating a shared vision and developing relationships with subordinates, while inspirational motivation is based on inspiring followers and setting highly desired expectations.

Leaders plan to execute business strategy to enhance

shareholder value, increase profitability, and motivate followers to meet the needs of customers. Intellectual stimulation on the other hand, facilitates knowledge sharing and generates more innovative solutions, while, individualized consideration, focuses on empowering employees and identifying their individual needs, which is directed at stimulating a learning workplace and mobilizing follower support toward organizational goals. [14]

Knowledge-oriented organizations blend both transformational leadership with knowledge management to increase follower satisfaction through the facilitation of knowledge and communication. Organizations are encouraged to develop transformational leaders through training and development to manifest a successful post-pandemic recovery. On the positive side of recovery, we see many organizations changing for the better as they build and disseminate the knowledge assets throughout all levels of organizations. According to scholars of the Harvard Business Review,

> "*Drawing on research from consulting firm Bain & Company, this article suggests that the pandemic has widened the gap between top performers and other companies in terms of the three main productivity drivers: people's time, their talent, and their energy.*" (Eric Garton and Michael Mankins, **The Pandemic Is**

Widening a Corporate Productivity Gap, December 2020).

We can see from this article that people's time, people's talent, and people's energy are a huge part of the successful post-pandemic recovery when time, talent, and energy are nurtured and used wisely.

Many organizations have embraced front-line workers working either as essential employees or actively working remotely, and this has added not only to their financial performance but also to employee satisfaction. This movement has improved organizational performance as people are recognized as vital to organizational success.

We found that various studies provided empirical evidence to support the vital importance of transformational leadership in improving the processes of knowledge management within organizations. [15] In addition to scholars, some CEOs have opined on the post-pandemic. Jamie Dimon of J. P. Morgan expresses his concern for the extenuating circumstances of remote work. Dimon has announced a bounce back strategy that may create a boom in the economy.

> *America's best-known banker thinks the U.S. economy is set to take off as the coronavirus abates. JPMorgan Chase CEO Jamie Dimon predicts in his annual letter to shareholders that widespread vaccinations, coupled*

*with more government spending and business reopening's, could propel the recovery for several years. (**JPMorgan Chase CEO Jamie Dimon says post-pandemic economic boom "could extend well into 2023"** Irina Ivanova, CBS News, April 7, 2021)*

As academic scholars and leadership practitioner's work together to sustain not only a successful business environment but also worker satisfaction, people return to work in droves. There still are several questions that are resonating today. Focusing on people, as noted above, coupled with business expansion forecasted by J. Dimon, we pose the following five questions that can help build a successful mindset in the post-pandemic recovery.

1. *What has influenced your way of thinking during the pandemic? Has your mindset changed?*
2. *How do you define your career now?*
3. *Is the mindset shift, if any, affecting your life?*
4. *Are there any behavioral or financial shifts that you have made?*
5. *What type of knowledge have you gained or feel that you are lacking based on the pandemic?*

Scholars illustrated that the four principal roles of transformational leaders have a direct, and in some cases, indirect impact on various financial and non-financial performance. The findings of these studies are summarized in the table below, (See Table 1). [16] [17]

Table 1: Effects of Transformational Leadership on Companies' Financial and Non-Financial Performance

The Principal Roles of Transformational Leaders	Financial Performance	Non-financial Performance
Idealized influence (Attributes)	Improving the price of stock	Post-Pandemic resilience
Idealized influence (Behaviors) and Inspirational motivation	Decreasing the costs of organization training and Development	Post-Pandemic survival
Intellectual stimulation And Individual considerations	Increasing organizational sales and improving service	Improving innovation
		Increasing rapid responses to environmental changes
		Improving the quality of products
		Improving customer focus
		Developing more

Post-Pandemic Recovery Approach

In a post-pandemic world, executives accumulate knowledge by creating new knowledge from organizational intellectual capital and acquiring knowledge from external environments such as but not limited to the Center for Disease Control, internal strategic analysis, and from customer relationship management. [18] The post-pandemic revealed new knowledge related to contingency planning which includes resilience. The exchange of knowledge with external business partners has developed into innovative environments that enable transformational leadership to create a more innovative platform for increased profitability in organizations. [19] [20] By creating a more innovative climate, executives have enhanced the capabilities of other leaders throughout the organization to act as inspirational motivators. Thus, the post-pandemic recovery has enabled all leaders in the organization to set high expectations in an effort to recognize possible opportunities in a chaotic global business environment.

Knowledge exchange in a post-pandemic world has contributed to transformational leadership. One way that transformational leaders facilitate this knowledge exchange is with idealized influence. The post-pandemic has led to the development of a more effective vision, including a more comprehensive array of information and insights about external environments based upon the new knowledge exchange that is indicative of safety and securing of not only the workforce, but for both clients and customers as well. This has led to a new look at resilience-strategy as organizations recovery from COVID-19.

Executives are responsible for knowledge integration which focuses on monitoring and evaluating knowledge management practices for their organization. They do this by coordinating the efforts of steering committees, sharing knowledge with the organization employees and customers, and continuously scanning the changes in technology. There are continuous updates in all industries regarding knowledge requirements to keep the quality of their production or services in-line with market demand. [18] For example, Moderna's chief executive said the COVID pandemic will come to an end in a year (DailyMail.co.uk, Emily Craig Health Reporter for Mailonone, 23 Sep 2021).

Knowledge integration activities can help leaders assess the required changes to keep the quality of both products and services at maximum levels, thus, improving performance and communication among stakeholders. A systematic process of coordinating company-wide experts, on steering committees, enables transformational leadership by propelling the role of intellectual stimulation, which creates a more innovative and creative environment to meet the needs of the post-pandemic recovery.

High-performing expert groups, as defined by Tiwana, Bharadwaj and Sambamurthy (2003), are considerably overlapped with Webb's (2007, p.54) empirical research that it is indicative of transformational leader trust. [21] [22] Trust in managing knowledge integration is examined by viewing the transformational leader capabilities in creating trust within companies. Mike Allen, President of Barry University, in Miami Florida, USA, mentioned, in an August 2019, at a University Assembly meeting, that organizations that can manifest information and distribute it timely and effectively throughout the organization by creating a model that is both efficient and effective will provide a platform for competitive advantage that will be tantamount to the industry and used worldwide for years to follow.

This idea of gathering information and distributing it timely has been manifested using flexible work groups that have implicated technical and knowledge-based support systems to help organizations not only recovery from the pandemic but also, in many cases, prosper.

We found that, in some cases, knowledge used within organizations may need to be reconfigured to meet environmental changes, new technological development, and new challenges that organization's face today.

"If you always do what you've always done, you'll always get what you've always got." — **Henry Ford**

What worked yesterday or a few years ago may have changed rapidly as technology is increasing in a prolific way. When common knowledge is successful, it is globally shared. There is a trickling down effect that takes time to reach the masses. For example, successful ideas and strategies with other organizations through domestic and global rewards such as the Malcolm Baldridge Award in the United States and the Deming Award in Japan, take time to manifest industries and progress may be much slower that necessary to meet the needs of our global environment. Even with new communication channels, past empirical studies have posited that companies might lack the required capabilities or decide to decline from interacting with other companies, or even suffer the distrust to share their knowledge. [23] [24] Reluctance among competitors to share best practices may impede progress in the post-pandemic world. This is nothing new. Knowledge sharing among companies in industries and people right in the same company are sometimes reluctant to share what they know. An article published in the Harvard Business Review titled "*Why Employees Don't Share Knowledge with Each Other*," by Marylène Gagné, Amy Wei Tian, Christine Soo, Bo Zhang, Khee Seng Benjamin Ho, and Katrina Hosszu, in July 19, 2019, express the reasoning behind this reluctance.

> Companies want employees to share what they know. Research has found that this leads to greater creativity, more innovation, and better performance, for individuals, teams, and organizations. Yet despite companies' attempts to encourage knowledge sharing (think of those open office spaces), many employees withhold what they know. They may play dumb, pretend not to know something, promise to share something but never do it, or tell people they can't share when in fact they could. New research finds that the way jobs are designed can affect whether employees share or hide knowledge from their colleagues. More cognitively complex jobs — in which people need to process large amounts of information and solve complex problems — tend to promote more knowledge sharing, as do jobs offering more autonomy. By focusing on these aspects of work, managers can encourage employees to share more and hide less. (HBR, 2019, Why Employees Don't Share Knowledge with Each Other)

The ability of an organization to recognize the new, external information, assimilate it, and apply it to commercial ends is critical for innovative capabilities. [25] Thus, limitations to distribute and the consent of receipt of knowledge, whether it be through a leader's own initiative, or caused by technology ineffectiveness, may lead to a stymied post-pandemic recovery.

The pandemic posed a reluctance to share knowledge in-person as many leaders lacked the ability to communicate as often as they did prior to the pandemic. Lee and Kim (2001) posit that the importance of networking, both positive and negative experiences, with business partners, is a key activity for organizations to enhance knowledge exchange. [18] As the post-pandemic unfolds, the impetus to initiate interaction that will benefit organizations and its stakeholders is imminent. We found that networking with external business partners may facilitate the role of idealized influence, thereby empowering transformational leaders to better develop strategic insights. With the vast array of knowledge sharing in the post-pandemic, executives are developing more effective missions and visions that incorporate various concerns and values with external business partners to work on a successful recovery plan.

> *The pandemic and corporate responses to it have shined a light on what is important in guiding a company's choices in the midst of the crisis. Many senior executives, partners, clients, and employees are seeing that robust social impact and sustainability programs are key to their firm's credibility—a community buy-in or acceptability akin to an unofficial "license to do business." This social commitment is*

crucial not just in good times, but perhaps even more important in times of crises. (Pamela Cone, 2020, ***The COVID-19 Pandemic: A Catalyst for Change in a New World***, Legal Business World)

We found that the knowledge transference among companies itself improves the effectiveness of learning, which in turn enables transformational leadership roles and its dimension, idealized consideration, to flourish, by empowering human resources and intellectual stimulation through creating new knowledge and solutions. [26]

Thus, these two key tenets of transformational leadership and knowledge management lead to a stronger opportunity for improved organizational performance. This construct is presented in Figure 1.

Knowledge Management

Transformational Leadership

Organizational Performance

While company performance is based on many external factors, we feel that knowledge management and transformational leadership may impact organizational performance as illustrated above. Networking within organizations and with people outside the organization can enhance the post-pandemic recovery.

We base our model, not only with our dialogue with leaders, but primarily on the empirical evidence pertaining to this by Lee and Choi (2003) and Oh (2009), which is indicative that knowledge is a significant indicator for improving organizational performance. [27] [28]

While these findings are decades old, these scholars emphasize how transformational leadership is used by top management executives and we have found that the application of this idea can impact the post-pandemic recovery.

Chapter Summary

Our simple model, transformational leadership plus knowledge management leading to organizational performance suggests that this coupling of the management processes may improve financial and non-financial performance through increased sales, improved customer and employee satisfaction, expansive learning opportunities, more innovation, and a higher quality product or service.

These links between and among knowledge management, transformational leadership, and organizational performance are crucial for the post-pandemic recovery. While further research is much needed in this area, we bring these three constructs, Transformational Leadership, Knowledge Management, and Organizational Performance together in a proposed model. We also extend the use of these three tenets to formulate a vision of improvement for the post-pandemic recovery.

Chapter 8: Operational Risk Management in The Post-Pandemic

*E*xecutives are spending more time today concerned about operational risk management than ever before. The reason for this is that we are experiencing an unprecedented time due to the COVID-19 pandemic.

Operational risk management, according to Karl Wiig, is an operational approach to represent knowledge management, and seeks to apply organizational knowledge in order to satisfy and exceed client expectations. Similar to customer relationship management, knowledge management is an enabler for identifying and satisfying customer needs and the idea manifests itself as a significant driver that motivates the development of relationships with customers.

Scholars have proven that executives can use knowledge management to improve customer satisfaction through acquiring additional knowledge from customers, developing better relationships with customers, and providing a higher quality of services and products. [2] [3]

As mentioned throughout this book, the key function of knowledge management is to help executives use it for employee development. [4] In this context, training is becoming the forefront of business success worldwide. Learning is a process that leads to acquiring new insights and knowledge, and potentially to correct sub-optimal or ineffective actions and behaviors that cause organizations to spiral out of control. [5]

Executives have found that encouraging organizational learning by codifying and modifying the behavior of employees, results in newer insight and knowledge. [6] Newer insights coupled with improved knowledge management can enhance the behaviors of followers to generate new knowledge, and is, therefore, a key factor in improving competitive advantage. [7]

Based on our experience of working with a team of top-level management consultants in the consulting industry, we found a positive grasp on the post-pandemic recovery and we see this continuing over the next five years. Our experience suggests that executives adding more manageable control coupled with increased private knowledge can not only reduce operational risk but also become more resilient. This idea of private knowledge, which refers to "a resource that is valuable, rare, and imperfectly imitable," is regarded as "firm-specific." [8] We found, from the executives we interviewed, that unique strategies, processes, and practices are examples of this type of knowledge. This type of knowledge in corporations must be guarded and not shared with the competition. Any leak of such information may increase the operational risk. Contrary to private knowledge, public knowledge differs in that it is not unique for any company. [8]

Public knowledge may be an asset and provide potential benefits when posted in social media and other means of communication. According to Sharon Matusik, public knowledge has been defined as "industry and occupational best practices" and is reflected in various concepts such as total quality management, six-sigma, and just-in-time inventory. [8] While some of these management fads have been shelved because of the pandemic, we feel that six sigma may be used more often while just-in-time inventory may become a thing of the past as some organizations are having supplier and production problems due to the pandemic. Total quality management, while still useful, is a thing of the past and some executives feel that it is management fad.

We found that the post-pandemic has caused executives to be more vigilant when considering the ownership of knowledge as a factor which is a significant contributor to the knowledge of organizations. Moreover, Sharon Matusik points out that knowledge emerges in two additional forms, including the knowledge that is only accessible by an organization and the knowledge that is accessible to all organizations. [8] The biggest concern, during the post-pandemic recovery, is coming up with a best practice approach to knowledge. The key to success for executives is to know which knowledge is to remain private and which to go public with. The latter being non-retractable which could have a larger impact on organizational performance. Thus, a mistake in this area may be vital to the organization and executives must choose wisely.

Internal resources manifest themselves in tangible (such as physical properties and machinery) and intangible (such as intellectual capital) forms. Intangible resources, in the form of intellectual capital, exist primarily as knowledge in human resources and cannot be easily imitated. This, by far, is why some organizations are successful at knowledge management and some are not. Operational risk, unlike resilience, is at risk if it can be easily imitated by the competition. Therefore, decreasing the imitability of services can also decrease the operational risk. Thus, making organizations harder to copy or imitate.

To remain competitive, executives realize that they must quickly create and share new ideas and knowledge to be more responsive to market changes. [9] Since organizations are "social communities that specialize in the creation and internal transfer of knowledge," this must remain a high priority. [10] The key concept to grasp is that knowledge, held by members of the organization, is the most strategic resource for competitive advantage, and its existence, use, and application through the way it is managed by executives can make or break an organization. [11] [12] [13]

Chapter Summary

The effective implementation of executive operational risk management requires developing knowledge management processes and the sharing of best practices and experiences among employees. This enhances overall organizational competitive advantage.

When executives ensure the effectiveness of knowledge management, they increase control and lessen operational risk. As a result, it is safe to say that private knowledge is essential for corporations while knowledge management, if not embraced can lead to operational risk and lack of resilience.

References

Chapter 1

[1] Sayyadi, M. & Provitera, M. (2021). The Post-Pandemic Recovery: Transformational Leadership and Knowledge Management, Fort Lauderdale, Florida: Motivational Leadership Training.

[2] Pisani, N. (2021). How COVID-19 Will Change the Geography of Competition. Sloan Management Review.

[3] Hasija, S., Padmanabhan, V. & Rampal P. (2020). Will the Pandemic Push Knowledge Work into the Gig Economy? Harvard Business Review.

[4] Carlsson-Szlezak, P., Reeves, M. & Swartz, P. (2020). What Coronavirus Could Mean for the Global Economy, Harvard Business Review.

[5] Carmichael, S.G. (2016). The Flash Report: The Global Digital Economy, Harvard Business Review.

[6] Carlsson-Szlezak, P., Swartz, P. & Reeves, M. (2020). Why The Global Economy Is Recovering Faster Than Expected, Harvard Business Review.

[7] Mokyr, J. (2020). Why Our Knowledge Economy Can Survive the New Age of Pestilence. Sloan Management Review.

[8] Kim, C. & Mauborgne, R. (2003). Fair Process: Managing in the Knowledge Economy, **Harvard Business Review.**

[9] Kim, C. & Mauborgne, R. (1999). Strategy, Value Innovation, and the Knowledge Economy, Sloan Management Review.

[10] Wong, K.Y. (2005). Critical Success Factors for Implementing Knowledge Management in Small and Medium Enterprises. Industrial Management & Data Systems, 105(3), 261-279.

[11] Hung, Y., Huang, S, Lin, Q., & Tsai, M. (2005). Critical factors in adopting a knowledge management systems for the pharmaceutical industry. Industrial Management & Data, 105(2), 164-183.

[12] Yeh, Y.J., Lai, S.Q., & Ho, C.T. (2006). Knowledge management enabler: a case study. Industrial Management & Data Systems, 106(6), 793-810.

[13] Migdadi, M. (2009). Knowledge management enablers and outcomes in the small-and-medium sized enterprises. Industrial Management & Data Systems, .109(6), 840-858.

[14] Lines, R., Selart, M., Espedal, B. and Johansen, S.T. (2005), "The production of trust during organizational change." Journal of Change Management, Vol. 5, No. 2, pp. 221–245.

[15] Ndlela, L. and Toit, A.D. (2001), "Establishing a knowledge management program for competitive advantage in an enterprise." International Journal of Information Management, Vol. 21, No. 2, pp. 151-165.

[16] Garvin, D.A. (1993), "Building a learning organization." Harvard Business Review, Vol. 71, No. 4, pp. 78–91.

[17] Zheng, W., Yang, B. and Mclean, G.N. (2010), "Linking organizational culture, structure, strategy, and organizational effectiveness: Mediating role of knowledge management." Journal of Business Research, Vol. 63, No. 7, pp. 763-771.

[18] Venkatraman, N. (1989), "Strategic orientation of business enterprises: the construct, dimensionality, and measurement." Management Science, Vol. 35, No. 8, pp. 942-962.

[19] Yang, J.T. (2004), "Qualitative knowledge capturing and organizational learning: two case studies in Taiwan hotels." Tourism Management, Vol. 25, No. 4, pp. 421-428.

[20] Zheng, W. (2005), "The impact of organizational culture, structure, and strategy on knowledge management effectiveness and organizational effectiveness." University of Minnesota, USA.

[21] Tsai, W. (2001), "Knowledge Transfer in Intraorganizational Networks: Effects of Network Position and Absorptive Capacity on Business Unit Innovation and Performance." The Academy of Management Journal, Vol. 44, No. 5, pp. 996-1004.

[22] Johnson J.L., Sohi R. and Grewal, R. (2004), "The Role of Relational Knowledge Stores in Interfirm Partnering." Journal of Marketing, Vol. 68, No. 3, pp. 21-36

[23] Hargadon, A.B. (1998), "Firms as Knowledge Broker: Lessons in Pursuing Continuous Innovation." California Management Review, Vol. 40, No. 3, pp. 209-227.

[24] Riege, A. and Lindsay, N. (2006), "Knowledge management in the public sector: stakeholder partnerships in the public policy development." Journal of Knowledge Management, Vol. 10, No. 3, pp. 24-39.

[25] Edelenbos, J., Van Buuren, A. and Van Schie, N. (2011), "Co-producing knowledge: joint knowledge production between experts, bureaucrats and stakeholders in Dutch water management projects." Environmental Science & Policy, Vol. 14, No. 6, pp. 675-684.

[26] Skyrme, D., & Amidon, D. (1997). The knowledge agenda. Journal of Knowledge Management, 1(1), 27-37.

[27] Trussler, S. (1999). The rules of the game In W. James, W. Cortada, & J.A Woods (Eds.), The knowledge Management Year Book 1999-2000, Boston: Butterworth-Heinemann.

[28] Liebowitz, J. (1999). Key Ingredients to the Success of an Organization's Knowledge Management Strategy. Knowledge and Process Management, 6(1), 37-40.

[29] APQC. (1999). Knowledge Management: Executive Summary (Consortium Benchmarking Study-Best Report). Houston: American Productivity & Quality Center.

[30] Holsapple, C., & Joshi, K.D. (2000). An investigation of factors that influence the management of knowledge in organizations. Journal of Strategic Information Systems, 9(2/3), 235-261.

[31] Stankosky, M., & Baldanza. C. (2001). A System Approach to Engineering a Knowledge Management System. In R.C. Barquin, A. Bennet and S. G. Remez. (Eds.), Knowledge Management: The Catalyst for Electronic Government, Virginia: Management Concepts.

[32] Wong, K.Y. (2005). Critical Success Factors for Implementing Knowledge Management in Small and Medium Enterprises. Industrial Management & Data Systems, 105(3), 261-279.

[33] Hung, Y., Huang, S, Lin, Q., & Tsai, M. (2005). Critical factors in adopting a knowledge management system for the pharmaceutical industry. Industrial Management & Data, 105(2), 164-183.

[34] Yeh, Y.J., Lai, S.Q., & Ho, C.T. (2006). Knowledge management enabler: a case study. Industrial Management & Data Systems, 106(6), 793-810.

[35] Migdadi, M. (2009). Knowledge management enablers and outcomes in the small-and-medium sized enterprises. Industrial Management & Data Systems, .109(6), 840-858.

Chapter 2

[1] O'Reilly, C.A. and Chatman, J.A. (1996). Culture as social control: Corporations, cults, and commitment. Research in Organizational Behavior, 18(7), 157-199.

[2] Balogun, J. and Jenkins, M. (2003). Re-conceiving Change Management: A Knowledge-based Perspective. European Management Journal, 21(2), 247-257.

[3] Scott, W.R. (2003). Organizations: Rational, nature, and open systems. Upper Saddle River, NJ: Prentice Hall.

[4] Eisenhardt, K. and Santos, F. (2006). Knowledge-based view: A new theory of strategy? in H. Pettigrew and T.R. Whittington, (Eds), Handbook of strategy and management (pp. 139-165), London, UK: SAGE Publications.

[5] Avolio, B.J., Waldman, D.A., & Yammariro, F.J. (1991). Leading in the 1990s: The Four I's of Transformational Leadership. Journal of European Industrial Training, 15(4), 9-16.

[6] Canty, L.T. (2005). Conceptual assessment: Transformational, transactional and laissez-faire leadership styles and job performances of managers as perceived by their direct reports (Unpublished doctoral dissertation) Capella University, USA.

[7] Marr, B., Gupta, O., Roos, G., & Pike, S. (2003). Intellectual Capital and Knowledge Management Effectiveness. Management Decision, 41(8), 771-781.

[8] Sayyadi, M. & Provitera, M. (2021). The Post-Pandemic Recovery: Transformational Leadership and Knowledge Management, Motivational Leadership Training, Fort Lauderdale, Florida, USA.

[9] Horwitz, I.B., Horwitz, S.K., Daram, P., Brandt, M.L., Brunicardi, F.C., & Awad, S.S. (2008). Transformational, transactional, and passive-avoidant leadership characteristics of a surgical resident cohort: analysis using the multifactor leadership questionnaire and implications for improving surgical education curriculums. The Journal of surgical research, 148(1), 49-59.

[10] Patiar, A., & Mia, L. (2009). Transformational leadership style, market competition and departmental performance: Evidence from luxury hotels in Australia. International Journal of Hospitality Management, 28(2), 254-262.

[11] Wenger, E.C. (1998). Communities of Practice. London: Cambridge University Press.

[12] Tafvelin, S. (2013). The transformational leadership process Retrieved from http://umu.diva-portal.org/smash/get/diva2:640843/FULLTEXT01.pdf.

[13] Sivadas, E., & Dwyer, F.R. (2000). An examination of organizational factors influencing new product success in internal and alliance-based processes. Journal of Marketing, 64(1), 31–50.

[14] Cardinal, L.B. (2001). Technological innovation in the pharmaceutical industry: the use of organizational control in managing research and development. Organization Science, 12(1), 19-36.

[15] Kasper, H., Muehlbacher, J., & Mueller B. (2006). The Effects of the Degree of Decentralization and Networks on Knowledge Sharing in MNCs Based on 6 Empirical Cases, Retrieved from http://www2.warwick.ac.uk/fac/soc/wbs/conf/olkc/archive /olkc1/papers/ 335_mueller.pdf.

[16] Cohen, M.D., & Sproull, L.S. (1996). Organizational Learning. Thousand Oaks, CA: Sage Publications.

[17] Talke, K. (2007). Corporate mindset of innovating firms: Influences on new product performance. Journal of Engineering and Technology Management, 24, 76-91.

[18] Zheng, W., Yang, B., & Mclean, G.N. (2010). Linking organizational culture, structure, strategy, and organizational effectiveness: Mediating role of knowledge management. Journal of Business Research, 63(7), 763-771.

Chapter 3

[1] Zheng, W. (2005). The impact of organizational culture, structure, and strategy on knowledge management effectiveness and organizational effectiveness (Unpublished PhD Thesis). University of Minnesota.

[2] Zheng, W., Yang, B. and Mclean, G.N. (2010). Linking organizational culture, structure, strategy, and organizational effectiveness: Mediating role of knowledge management. Journal of Business Research, 63(7), 763-771.

[3] Reus, T.H. (2004). A knowledge-based view of international acquisition performance (Unpublished PhD Thesis). The Florida State University.

[4] Darroch, J. (2005). Knowledge management, innovation and firm performance. Journal of Knowledge Management, 9(3), 101 – 115.

[5] Wu, I.L. and Chen J.L. (2014). Knowledge management driven firm performance: the roles of business process capabilities and organizational learning. Journal of Knowledge Management, 18(6), 1141 – 1164.

[6] Birasnav, M. (2014). Knowledge management and organizational performance in the service industry: The role of transformational leadership beyond the effects of transactional leadership. Journal of Business Research, Vol. 67, No. 8, pp. 1622-1629.

[7] Politis, J. D. (2001). The relationship of various leadership styles on knowledge management. Leadership & Organizational Development Journal, Vol. 22, No. 7/8, pp. 354- 365

[8] Eom, M., Kahai, S., & Yayla, A. (2015). Investigation of How IT Leadership Impacts IT-Business Alignment through Shared Domain Knowledge and knowledge Integration. https://pdfs.semanticscholar.org/c150/38187023e0d3fc53da1fdf359f5d1386352d.pdf

[9] Lin, R.S., & Hsiao, J.K. (2014). The Relationships between Transformational Leadership, Knowledge Sharing, Trust and Organizational Citizenship Behavior. International Journal of Innovation, Management and Technology, Vol. 5, No. 3, pp. 171-174.

[10] Liu, Y., & Phillips, J.S. (2011). Examining the antecedents of knowledge sharing in facilitating team innovativeness from a multilevel perspective. International Journal of Information Management, Vol. 31, No. 1, pp. 44-52

[11] Noseworthy, S. (1998). Transformational leadership and information technology: implications for secondary school Leaders PhD Thesis. Memorial University of Newfoundland, Canada.

[12] Yee, D. (2000). Images of school principals' information and communications technology leadership. Journal of Information Technology for teacher Education, Vol. 9, No. 3, pp. 287-302.

[13] Schepers, J., Wetzels, M., & de Ruyter, K. (2005). Leadership styles in technology acceptance. Journal of Managing Service Quality, Vol. 15, No. 6, pp. 496-508.

Chapter 4

[1] Anand, A., & Singh M.D. (2011). Understanding Knowledge Management: a literature review. International Journal of Engineering Science and Technology, Vol. 3, No. 2, pp. 926-939.

[2] Barney, J.B. (1991). Firm Resources and Sustained Competitive Advantage. Journal of Management, Vol. 17, No. 1, pp. 99-120.

[3] Gold, A.H., Malhotra, A., & Segars, A.H. (2001). Knowledge Management: An Organizational Capabilities Perspective. Journal of Management Information Systems, Vol. 18, No. 1, pp. 185-214.

[4] Grant, R.M. (1996). Toward a Knowledge-based Theory of the Firm. Strategic Management Journal, Vol. 17, No. S2, pp. 109-122.

[5] Jessup, L. M., Connoly, T., and Galegher, J. (1990). The Effects of Anonymity on GDSS. MSI Quarterly, 14 (3), pp. 313-321.

Chapter 5

[1] Bergeron, F., Raymond, L., & Rivard, S. (2004). Ideal patterns of strategic alignment and business

performance. Information & management, 41(8), 1003-1020.

[2] Venkatraman, N. (1989). Strategic orientation of business enterprises: the construct, dimensionality, and measurement. Management Science, 35(8), 942-962.

[3] Zheng, W. (2005). The impact of organizational culture, structure, and strategy on knowledge management effectiveness and organizational effectiveness [Unpublished doctoral dissertation]. University of Minnesota.

[4] Zheng, W., Yang, B., & Mclean, G.N. (2010). Linking organizational culture, structure, strategy, and organizational effectiveness: Mediating role of knowledge management. Journal of Business Research, 63(7), 763-771.

Chapter 6

[1] Bass, B.M. (1999). Two Decades of Research and Development in Transformational Leadership. European Journal of Work and Organization, Vol. 8, No. 1, pp. 9-32.

[2] Darling, S.K. (1990). A study to identify and analyze the relationship between (1) transformational leadership and collaboration, and (2) transactional leadership and collaboration in selected Minnesota elementary schools, Unpublished PhD Thesis). University of Minnesota.

[3] Bass, B.M., & Steidlmeier, P. (1999). Ethics, Character, and Authentic Transformational Leadership Behavior. Leadership Quarterly, Vol. 10, No. 2, pp. 181-218.

[4] Bass, B.M. and Avolio, B.J. (1997), Full range leadership development: Manual for the Multifactor Leadership Questionnaire, MindGarden, California, CA.

[5] Meindl, J.R. and Ehrlich, S.B. (1987), The Romance of Leadership and the Evaluation of Organizational Performance, Academy of Management Journal, Vol. 30, No. 1, pp. 91-109.

[6] Garvin, D. (1988). Managing quality: The strategic and competitive edge, Free Press, New York, NY.

[7] Hancott, D.E. (2005). The relationship between transformational leadership and organizational performance in the largest public companies in Canada, Unpublished Doctoral Dissertation. Capella University.

[8] Zhu, W., Chew, I.K., and Spangler, W.D. (2005). CEO transformational leadership and organizational outcomes: The mediating role of human capital-enhancing human resource management. The Leadership Quarterly, Vol. 16, No. 1, pp. 39-52.

[9] García-Morales V.J., Matías-Reche, F and Hurtado-Torres, N. (2008). Influence of transformational leadership on organizational innovation and performance depending on the level of organizational learning in the pharmaceutical sector. Journal of Organizational Change Management, Vol. 21, No. 2, pp. 188 – 212.

[10] Bertsch, D.L. (2009), The relationship between transformational and transactional leadership of symphony orchestra conductors and organizational performance in U.S. symphony orchestras, Unpublished Doctoral Dissertation, Capella University.

[11] Flemming, P.L. (2009). A study of the relationship between transformational leadership traits and organizational culture types in improving performance in public sector organizations: A Caribbean perspective, Unpublished Doctoral Dissertation, Capella University.

[12] Patiar, A., and Mia, L. (2009). Transformational leadership style, market competition and departmental performance: Evidence from luxury hotels in Australia. International Journal of Hospitality Management, Vol. 28, No. 2, pp. 254-262.

[13] Cho, T. (2011), Knowledge management capabilities and organizational performance: An investigation into the effects of knowledge infrastructure and processes on organizational performance, PhD Thesis, University of Illinois at Urbana-Champaign.

[14] MacNeil, C.M. (2003). Line managers: facilitators of knowledge sharing in teams. Employee Relations, Vol. 25, No. 3, pp. 294-307.

[15] Girard, J.P. (2006). Where is the knowledge we have lost in managers? Journal of Knowledge Management, Vol. 10, No. 6, pp. 22-38.

[16] Jain A.K., and Jeppesen, H.J. (2013). Knowledge management practices in a public sector organization: The role of leaders' cognitive styles. Journal of Knowledge Management, Vol. 17, No. 3, pp. 347-362.

[17] Deshpande, R. (1982). The organizational context of market research use. Journal of Marketing, Vol. 46, No. 4, pp. 91-101.

[18] Bass, B., and Avolio, B. (2004). Multifactor Leadership Questionnaire Manual. Mind Garden, Inc., Menlo Park, CA.

Chapter 7

[1] Polanyi, M. (1966), The Tacit Dimension, Routledge, London.

[2] Kostova, T. and Roth, K. (2002), "Adoption of an Organizational Practice by Subsidiaries of Multinational Corporations: Institutional and Relational Effects", Academy of Management Journal, Vol. 45, No. 1, pp. 215-233.

[3] Inkpen, A.C. and Tsang, E.W.K. (2005), "Social Capital, Networks, and Knowledge Transfer", Academy of Management Review, Vol. 30, No. 1, pp. 146-165.

[4] Li, L. (2005), "The effects of trust and shared vision on inward knowledge transfer in subsidiaries' intra- and inter-organizational relationships", International business review, Vol. 14, No. 1, pp. 77-95.

[5] Wasko, M.M. and Faraj, S. (2005), "Why Should I Share? Examining Social Capital and Knowledge Contribution in Electronic Networks of Practice", MIS Quarterly, Vol. 29, No. 1, pp. 35-57.

[6] Kogut B. and Zander. U. (1996), "What do firms do? Coordination identity and learning", Organization Science, Vol. 7, No. 5, pp. 502-518.

[7] Nonaka, I. and Takeuchi, H. (1995), The knowledge-creating company: how Japanese companies create the dynamics of innovation, Oxford University Press, New York, NY.

[8] Brown, J.S. and Duguid, P. (2000), The social life of information, Harvard Business School Press, Boston, MA.

[9] Gordon, C.M. (2002), "Contributions of cultural anthropology and social capital theory to understandings of knowledge management", PhD Thesis, University of Toronto.

[10] Bass, B.M. and Steidlmeier, P. (1999), "Ethics, Character, and Authentic Transformational Leadership Behavior", Leadership Quarterly, Vol. 10, No. 2, pp. 181-218.

[11] Pemberton, J., Mavin, S. and Stalker, B. (2007), "Scratching beneath the surface of communities of (mal)practice", Learning Organization, Vol. 14, No. 1, pp. 62-73.

[12] Braga, D. (2002), "Transformational leadership attributes as perceived by team members of knowledge networks", PhD Thesis, Pepperdine University.

[13] Webb, K. (2007), "Motivating peak performance: Leadership behaviors that stimulate employee motivation and performance", Christian Higher Education, Vol. 6, No. 1, pp. 53-71.

[14] Lowe, K.B., Kroeck, K.G. and Sivasubramaniam, N. (1996), "Effectiveness correlates of transformational and transactional leadership: A meta-analytic review of the LMQ literature." Leadership Quarterly, Vol. 7, No. 3, pp. 385-415.

[15] Liu, Y. and Phillips, J.S. (2011), "Examining the antecedents of knowledge sharing in facilitating team innovativeness from a multilevel perspective." International Journal of Information Management, Vol. 31, No. 1, pp. 44-52.

[16] Hancott, D.E. (2005), "The relationship between transformational leadership and organizational performance in the largest public companies in Canada." Capella University, USA.

[17] García-Morales, V.J., Jiménez-Barrionuevo, M.M. and Gutiérrez-Gutiérrez, L. (2012), "Transformational leadership influence on organizational performance through organizational learning and innovation." Journal of Business Research, Vol. 65, No. 7, pp. 1040-1050.

[18] Lee, J.H. and Kim, Y.G. (2001), "A stage model of organizational knowledge management: a latent content analysis." Expert Systems with Applications, Vol. 20, No. 4, pp. 299-311.

[19] Wang, Z. and Wang, N. (2012), "Knowledge sharing, innovation and firm performance." Expert Systems With Applications, Vol. 39, No. 10, pp. 8899-8908.

[20] Canty, L.T. (2005), "Conceptual assessment: Transformational, transactional and laissez-faire leadership styles and job performances of managers as perceived by their direct reports." Capella University, USA.

[21] Tiwana, A., Bharadwaj, A. and Sambamurthy, V. (2003), The Antecedents of Information Systems Development Capability in Firms: A Knowledge Integration Perspective, Proceedings of Twenty-Fourth International Conference on Information Systems, 2003, Seattle, Washington, pp. 21-33.

[22] Webb, K. (2007), "Motivating peak performance: Leadership behaviors that stimulate employee motivation and performance." Christian Higher Education, Vol. 6, No. 1, pp. 53-71.

[23] Caldwell, D.F. and Ancona, D.G. (1988), "Beyond Task and Maintenance." Group & Organization Management, Vol. 13, No. 4, pp. 468-494.

[24] Kraut, R. and Streeter, L. (1995), "Coordination in software development." Communications of the ACM, Vol. 38, No. 3, pp. 69-81.

[25] Cohen, W.M. and Levinthal, D.A. (1990), "Absorptive Capacity: A New Perspective on Learning and Innovation." Administrative Science Quarterly, Vol. 35, No. 1, pp. 128-152.

[26] Purvis, R.L., Sambamurthy, V. and Zmud R.W. (2000), "The development of knowledge embeddedness in CASE technologies within organizations." IEEE Transactions on Engineering Management, Vol. 47, No. 2, pp. 245-257.

[27] Lee, H. and Choi B. (2003), "Knowledge management enablers, processes, and organizational performance: an integrative view and empirical examination." Journal of Management Information Systems, Vol. 20, No. 1, pp. 179-228.

[28] Oh, S.Y. (2009), "The relationship between quality management, organizational learning, and organizational performance." University of Illinois at Urbana, USA.

Chapter 8

[1] Wiig, K.M. (1994). Knowledge management foundations: Thinking about thinking- How people and organizations create, represent, and use knowledge. Arlington, Texas: Schema Press.

[2] North K., Reinhardt, R., & Schmidt A. (2004). The Benefits of Knowledge Management: Some empirical evidence. v Retrieved from http://www2.warwick.ac.uk/fac/soc/wbs/ conf/olkc/archive /oklc5/papers/a-8_north.pdf.

[3] Sukumaran, S., Sukumaran, S., Shetty, M.V., & Shetty, M.V. (2009). Knowledge Management (KM) in automobile: Application of a value chain (VC) approach using KM tools, Retrieved from http://ieeexplore.ieee.org/stamp/stamp.jsp?arnumber=0 54025 54.

[4] Spender, J.C. (1996). Organizational knowledge, learning and memory: three concepts in search of a theory. Journal of Organizational Change Management, 9(1), 63-78.

[5] Dorfler, V. (2010). Learning capability: the effect of existing knowledge on learning. Knowledge Management Research & Practice, 8, 369–379.

[6] Aulakh, P.S., Kundu, S.K., & Lahiri, S. (2016). Learning and knowledge management in and out of emerging markets: Introduction to the special issue. 51(5), 655-661.

[7] Linderman, K., Schoeder, R.G., Zaheer, S., Liedtke, C., & Choo, A.S. (2004). Integrating quality management practices with knowledge creation processes. Journal of Operations Management, 22(6), 589-607.

[8] Matusik, S.F. (1998). The Utilization of Contingent Work, Knowledge Creation, and Competitive Advantage. The Academy of Management Review, 23(4), 680-697.

[9] Eisenhardt, K., & Santos, F. (2006). Knowledge-based view: A new theory of strategy? In H. Pettigrew, & T.R. Whittington (Eds.), Handbook of strategy and management, London: Sage Publications Ltd.

[10] Kogut, B., & Zander, U. (1993). Knowledge of the firm and the evolutionary theory of the multinational corporation. Journal of International Business Studies, 24(4), 625-645.

[11] Kogut, B., & Zander, U. (1992). Knowledge of the firm, combinative capabilities, and the replication of technology. Organization Science, 3, 383-397.

[12] De Carolis, D. (2002). The Role of Social Capital and Organizational Knowledge in Enhancing Entrepreneurial Opportunities in High-Technology Environments, In Choo & Bontis (Eds.) The Strategic Management of Intellectual Capital and Organizational Knowledge, New York: Oxford University Press.

[13] Curado, C. (2006). The knowledge based-view of the firm: from theoretical origins to future implications. Retrieved from http://citeseerx.ist.psu.edu/viewdoc/download?doi=10.1.1.322.8178&rep=rep1&type=pdf.

Featured Case Study

Tesla, A Knowledge Management Think Tank

Dr. Michael J. Providera, Management Consultant, Business Book Author, Management Professor
Published 9-11-2021 (All Rights Reserved)
Copyright ®Dr. Michael J. Providera September 11, 2021
Copy only with permission by the author (email, website)
docprov@msn.com
http://docprov.com

Jeanty Remy, known as Remy, ran out of his home office with a staggering leap. He was on his work-from-home day which is three out of five; he is a nurse-practitioner and entrepreneur in Miami, Florida, USA, and he spends two days at the office and works from home remotely the other three days. He is a single Dad that drives his daughters to school every day. It was 6:30 am and he was heading into the dark sunrise with his daughter Tameka whom he was taking to school.

Remy was contemplating buying a Tesla because he was clocking so many miles each week. His girlfriend, Wendy, lived two-hours away in Naples, Florida, and the cost of gas was burdensome. Costco premium was topping at 3.29$ a gallon, and his Jaguar was punching about 28 miles per gallon on the highway. A typical Saturday to Sunday week of driving would cost close to 100$. Electric cars may rack up 19$ in spark for the same distance. Remy loved his Jag, but reality was beginning to set in, and the electric car was calling him. Besides, his 19-year-old daughter, Alexa, loves the Tesla. Yep, she loved everything about it. From the way the car drives to the expansive technology to the gaming capability.

He thought about a Hybrid and investigated the local Lexus dealer, found one certified. Spoke to a salesperson about the car in mind. The car of interest, clocking in at 39 miles per gallon highway and 40 miles per gallon city, Remy thought he should look. After turning down an appointment with the salesperson he spoke to that day, Remy drove to the dealer anyway. He felt that the Hybrid Lexus was not meant to be. Well, he got to the Lexus dealer and the car was not showing. The salespeople were all busy looking at computer screens and meeting with customers. There was such an abundance of cars that the thought of digging out the one of interest was a long shot. Remy thought the car was up front and that he can view it immediately. Not the case and there were cars everywhere. No shortage of cars at this dealership. Remy said to himself "Even if I bought the car, it would only save me about 30% in gas each week." The fact that he did not have to plug it in was the draw. However, going 100% electric was still calling him The Lexus, while great cars (the newer hybrid was getting 44 miles per gallon), lead to a short-lived experience.

The Tesla Corporation

The Knowledge management at Tesla is what Remy would call "State of the Art." Here is Remy's idea of how Tesla meets the demands of a Knowledge Management System:
1) Tesla provides the buyer less time searching for information because it is all on the website page with only a few options (automobile color option @ 2,000$, Full-Self Driving @ 10,000, etc.)
2) Tesla offers the customer less time asking for information with the no haggle pricing of vehicles
3) Team Tesla is super responsive (i.e., instantaneous financing option at 2.49% with a personal credit rating of 650 or higher)
4) Tesla employees are all one-team working together to support the customer experience

5) Tesla provides an internet dashboard that states your personalized page for each customer with detailed information to support the purchase of the vehicle and accessories. (i.e., Remy's Tesla)
6) Tesla offers continuous customer learning experience about features and purchase options with comparison to fuel-injected vehicles
7) Tesla's knowledge management helps the organization as one big "Tesla family," including customers
8) Tesla does not place unnecessary pressure on customers as the customer-knowledge about the car-buying process unfolds
9) Tesla uses knowledge management as a precursor to let the ***buyer beware*** of the state-of-the-art of electric vehicles
10) Tesla does not ask from large sums of money upfront and does not persuade the customer, in any way, to buy the car, which builds a true knowledge management customer service system based on real-time data

One advisor at Tesla told Remy. If you buy a car in May, in any given year, and a new type of light technology is discovered, the light is installed on the newer cars and your car is left behind on that implementation, unfortunately. However, when a software update is available, your car is immediately updated at no charge.

At the Tesla corporation, strategic objectives are constantly being tweaked to include supplier support and vendor relationships as the world manages the post-pandemic recovery.

The primary function of knowledge management is to restructure unclear and vague situations into a set of organizationally resolvable problems. Solutions are key to Tesla's success as the pandemic evolves. Thus, Tesla's Knowledge Management is implemented and formulated to efficiently deploy the organizational capabilities and interact with the global environment.

Remy's Options

Remy is sticking with the Tesla Model 3 Long Range, which has the capacity to go about 350 miles on one charge. He knows that other car manufacturers are attempting to not only catch up but surpass Tesla Motor Corporation technology. The American made Tesla car is still producing a better, more responsive battery, but how long can this last.

> Tesla, with the stock ticker (TSLA) currently has a very clear technological lead over its competitors. One teardown in 2020 estimated it to be six years ahead of Toyota and VW. There seems no stopping the share price of the company either. In fact, Tesla doesn't just have a higher market cap than Toyota, it's nearly four times as much now and recently passed Facebook to become the fifth most valuable US company. But although Tesla is awash with investor cash and producing cars that have significantly more range and performance than other vendors, there are signs already that its market lead is eroding, and competitors are starting to catch up. (James Morris, 2021, ***Tesla's Dominance Could Be Under Threat Sooner Than You Think,*** Forbes*)*

Right now, Remy feels that similar to customer relationship management, knowledge management is an enabler for identifying and satisfying customer's needs and the idea manifests itself as a significant driver that motivates the development of relationships with customers. Remy feels that searching further, at this time, is not an option for him.

With automobile chips on hold and scarce to come by, Remy realizes production of his new vehicle is the only option. He cannot afford the S-class Tesla, which is 85,000$, not including the 10,000$ software upgrade for Full Self-Driving Capability.

Remy feels that Tesla is creating a conducive organizational climate that fosters knowledge management which, he feels, is not only the key to post-pandemic recovery, but also the best way to solve his financial crunch due to the cost of gas and his driving status.

The Deal

Sunrise unfolded nicely as Remy drove to work, arriving at his office at 7:30 am. By lunch time, Remy was set upon buying a Tesla. He asked his daughter Alexa, who was at the office that day, if she thought it was a good idea to buy a Tesla. Alexa said, "Dad, it's expensive. A huge investment, sure I would love a Tesla but you sure you want to do it?" "Yes, Alexa, gas is costing me too much and I am racking up miles each week which will bring the value of my Jaguar down substantially, besides, I come out of warranty in May of 2022 and that is only about 7 months away," Remy replied.

Remy called the Tesla team and got a voice. Amber, at Tesla, was nice and helpful. She mentioned that there are no cars in the Florida area with the specifics that Remy desired. She located a car in Atlanta and gave Remy the zip code and told him to go to the Tesla website and search with the Atlanta zip. Remy did and found it. A black Tesla with white interior, a 2021model 3 long range, Tesla. White interior was a 1,000$ upgrade and Amber did not tell Remy, but the color black was an upgrade also, $2,000. The car was priced at 51,000$, plus an optional software upgrade of 10,000$ for Full-Self-Driving Capability. The car was a demo because it had 3,000 miles on it. The price adjustment for the miles is 784$. The car had to be picked up in Atlanta, however, a ten-hour drive. Remy agreed, paid the 250$ online fee and bought the car. Yep, Remy bought a 61,000$ car, online, with no salespeople engaged. Once he bought it, more screens came up to finalize the purchase. Cash, finance, or lease was an option, and Remy wanted to finance with some money down to lower his coupon payment. He filled out a quick form and instantly, less than 30 seconds, he got a text message on his phone with approved financing from a Bank that he never heard of but was happy to do business with them.

Text Message: Financing for your Tesla has been approved. Go to your Tesla account for more details.

Next day text message from the Tesla advisor: Hi Remy, welcome to the Tesla family! Go to your account to get started on your pre-delivery tasks.
Remy's phone began to ring and another representative from Tesla wanted to congratulate and talk to him about the new car purchase. She mentioned that he had to pick up the car in four days. This all happen so suddenly. Luckily, Remy was on his lunch hour and was not in a meeting.
"What," Remy stated back in a text message to the Tesla advisor. "I am working, driving my children, and I do not even have a free weekend this week." The represented said "That is the deal, you can see the specifics on your dashboard. Sure enough, it states: Estimated Delivery: September 21 – September 24. A four-day window and it is Tuesday, so pick up time is Friday, ten hours away, without a weekend to travel.

The trade in of the Jaguar was another issue that had to be sorted out. Kee, the Tesla advisor, mentioned that she would help. She texted back shortly with an estimated trade in value of $19,329. Remy thought this was low because the Kelly Blue Book mid-range was about 22,000$. The next day, Remy visited the Carvana website, and he got an instant quote of 25,000$. It appeared in seconds, with a pickup date in 2 days at his home. Obviously, there was some leeway in the trade in value with that large of a margin. "Trading a car in saves on taxes on the new car," Remy thought.

Flying High in April Shot Down in May

It was 1PM and Remy owned a Tesla with a down payment on a credit card of 250$. Remy told Tameka that he just bought the car but had to go to Atlanta to pick it up. She said "Atlanta?" Remy replied, "Yes, I am not sure if I can swing it."

He texted a picture to Tameka, who was at school, and said I bought the Tesla. Tameka replied "Wow, Dad, that is amazing."

After watching some videos on youtube.com, Remy decided to call the representative to inquire about the wear and tear of the Tesla car because it is a demo with 3,000 miles on it. The representative mentioned that you will be buying the car "As Is." Remy said, "What, I noticed a video that mentioned that some Tesla's rattle and they may also have a seat cushion disfunction. What happens then? Am I covered for that?"

"Unfortunately, not, because you are buying the car used and that is not covered," the representative mentioned.

Remy, now baffled, called off the deal because he could not make it to Atlanta within the timeframe and even another day would not work since it is a ten-hour drive one way, and he was running a motivational seminar on Saturday. Keeping his money in the game, he thought he would wait and see what happens.

After further contemplation, Remy decided to buy brand and build his Tesla model to order. He put that in motion. His delivery window was November to December 2021. Pick up in Ft. Lauderdale. Sweet!

Reflecting on Remy's Motivation

"I am quick to make decisions and never look an opportunity with a shy eye," Remy always said about his motivation, and most of all, "I love to go beyond the status quo and do more and work as hard as I can to provide for my children." With two kids in private school, times were tough for him, but Remy did his best to ensure his children were happy and well educated. Cutting down his huge gasoline expense may help relieve some of his financial burden. He always tries to lead his children with optimism. Robert Iger, CEO of Walt Disney Corporation, quotes:

Optimism is a very very important part of leadership. People don't like to follow pessimists. -Robert Iger

This was Remy's focus to always remain positive. Remy has a plague in his office by L. P. Jacks that said:

> *A master in the art of living draws no sharp distinction between his work and his play; his labor and his leisure; his mind and his body; his education and his recreation. He hardly knows which is which. He simply pursues his vision of excellence through whatever he is doing, and leaves others to determine whether he is working or playing. To himself, he always appears to be doing both.*

Alexa asked Remy if the Tesla was a go and Remy responded with a delayed look on his face, "Probably not, definitely not right now." Alexa was disappointed but understood the logistics of the Atlanta deal. Remy told his daughters to always go out and get what you desire. He remembered a quote of a great leader and kept this saying on his desk at work:

> *"Be who…you were meant to be, and you will set the world on fire."*

The Tesla Journey had Pitfalls

Remy decided to build his Tesla and take delivery in the November-December window. Thinking of a new car coming in around thanksgiving and Christmas was somewhat exciting. He thought to himself "I wonder when the new Tesla in 2022 will roll out, probably August 2022," he thought.

He asked the representative via text, "When do the 2022s come out in mid-year?"

The representative responded, "It is a slightly different with Tesla – Any car made Jan 1, 22 will be a 2022. They are not changing from our 2021's. Hope that answers the question."

That helps, texted Remy. He also asked, "will the price change?" He did not receive a response.

Its September 24, 2021, Remy must make his purchase decision now. Delivery of a 2021 model 3 Tesla will be delivered in Fort Lauderdale, Florida, USA, with a November-December window. Lots to think about for Remy but a decision must be made, today.

Discussion Questions:

1. Is Remy making the right decision by buying a Tesla? Should he have the car delivered in the November/December window? Should he pay for the 10,000$ upgrade or purchase that later?
2. How effective is Tesla corporation at Knowledge Management?
3. Can you share your knowledge about Tesla, the organization's global reach, or its stock price?
4. What are the advantages and disadvantages between a Hybrid and an electric car?
5. What kind of car do you drive? Would you consider an electric car? Is gas, miles per hour, oil changes, and wear and tear a burden to you or do you take it in stride because you love your car?

Michael Provitera, Assistant Professor of Organizational Behavior at Barry University, Miami, Florida, USA, prepared this case based on the post-pandemic recovery of the automobile industry as the basis of class discussion at both the graduate and undergraduate level, for business school, rather than to illustrate either effective or ineffective handling of an automobile sale. The case is based on the purchase of a modern state-of-the-art electric car called

"Tesla," and the company is a publicly traded organization on the New York Stock Exchange with the stock ticker of TSLA. This case study is not a view of actual details and all the information is fictitious and created to encourage discussion-learning about the automobile industry. No permission to publish this case has been granted by the Tesla Corporation and this is not a positive or negative representation of a car-buying process. This case study should not encourage the buy or sale of a Tesla or its stock and is written for educational purposes only. For further information regarding this case, please contact the author at docprov@msn.com.

About the Author

Michael Provitera is a Management Trainer and Associate Professor of Organizational Behavior at Barry University in Miami, Florida USA. He prepared this case based on fictitious information and some actual events that took place in his fifteen-year career as an executive in the financial industry. The case is unique for leadership and management discussion learning as the basis of classroom [or training] discussion at both the graduate and undergraduate level [and executive seminars] rather than to illustrate either effective or ineffective handling of an administrative or personal career or leadership situation. The case is based on leadership ideas and creative assumptions made without reference or permission of the people named [all names are made up unless otherwise stated]. For further information regarding this case or for permission to use it in the classroom or for corporate training, contact the author, Dr. Michael Provitera, at **docprov@msn.com** *or visit the author's website at http://docprov.com.*

***

About the Authors

Michael J. Provitera is an executive leadership trainer. As president of Motivational Leadership Training, his focus is on improving organizational effectiveness and enhancing individual success. He has trained over 1000 executives. His executive leadership certification runs eighteen hours and covers six factors of leadership. A new specialized three-hour executive certification is now available. His clients have been Pfizer, Trane, Interval International, and the City of North Miami. Michael is sought by reporters for quotes in prominent media such as Forbes, US New & World Report, The Daily News, Fox Business, Higher Ed Jobs, Hr.com, NBC News, and The Washington Times. The author can be contacted at: docprov@msn.com.

Mostafa Sayyadi is an international management consultant. He works with senior business leaders to effectively develop innovation in companies and helps companies—from start-ups to the Fortune 100—succeed by improving the effectiveness of their leaders. He is a business book author and a long-time contributor to HR.com, Conscious Company Magazine, The Canadian Business Journal and Consulting Magazine and his work has been featured in these top-flight business publications. In recognition of his work with Australian Institute of Management and Australian Human Resources Institute, he has been awarded the titles, "Associate Fellow of the Australian Institute of Management" and "Senior Professional in Human Resources." The author can be contacted at: mostafasayyadi1@gmail.Com.

www.ingramcontent.com/pod-product-compliance
Lightning Source LLC
Chambersburg PA
CBHW031417210526
45464CB00005B/1930